THE MANAGER POOL

The Software Patterns Series

Series Editor: John M. Vlissides

The Software Patterns Series (SPS) comprises pattern literature of lasting significance to software developers. Software patterns document general solutions to recurring problems in all software-related spheres, from the technology itself, to the organizations that develop and distribute it, to the people who use it. Books in the series distill experience from one or more of these areas into a form that software professionals can apply immediately. *Relevance* and *impact* are the tenets of the SPS. Relevance means each book presents patterns that solve real problems. Patterns worthy of the name are intrinsically relevant; they are borne of practitioners' experiences, not theory or speculation. Patterns have impact when they change how people work for the better. A book becomes a part of the series not just because it embraces these tenets, but because it has demonstrated it fulfills them for its audience.

Titles in the series:

The Design Patterns Smalltalk Companion, Sherman Alpert/Kyle Brown/Bobby Woolf

The Joy of Patterns: Using Patterns for Enterprise Development, Brandon Goldfedder

The Manager Pool: Patterns for Radical Leadership, Don Olson/Carol Stimmel

The Pattern Almanac 2000, Linda Rising

Pattern Hatching: Design Patterns Applied, John Vlissides

Pattern Languages of Program Design, edited by James O. Coplien/Douglas C. Schmidt

Pattern Languages of Program Design 2, edited by John M. Vlissides/James O. Coplien/ Norman L. Kerth

Pattern Languages of Program Design 3, edited by Robert Martin/Dirk Riehle/ Frank Buschmann

Pattern Languages of Program Design 4, edited by Neil Harrison/Brian Foote/ Hans Rohnert

Small Memory Software, James Noble/Charles Weir

Please see our web site at http://www.awl.com/cseng/swpatterns
for more information on these titles.

THE
MANAGER
POOL

Patterns for Radical Leadership

DON SHERWOOD OLSON
and CAROL L. STIMMEL

ADDISON-WESLEY

Boston • San Francisco • New York • Toronto • Montreal
London • Munich • Paris • Madrid
Capetown • Sydney • Tokyo • Singapore • Mexico City

The publisher offers discounts on this book when ordered for special sales. For more information, please contact:

Pearson Education Corporate Sales Division
One Lake Street
Upper Saddle River , NJ 07458
(800) 382-3419
corpsales@pearsontechgroup.com

Visit AW on the Web: www.awl.com/cseng/

Library of Congress Cataloging-in-Publication Data

Olson, Don, 1951–
    The manager pool : patterns for radical leadership / Olson, Don [and] Stimmel, Carol.
       p.   cm.
    Includes bibliographical references and index.
    ISBN 0-201-72583-5
    1. Executives.   2. Executive ability.   3. Leadership.   4. High technology industries—
Management. I. Stimmel, Carol. II. Title.

   HD38.2 .O45 2001
   658.4'092—dc21   2001046248

0-201-72583-X
Text printed on recycled paper
1 2 3 4 5 6 7 8 9 10—SPS—0504030201
First printing, October 2001

For Robin and our son Jake, who reminded me that it was time to begin my life—C.S.
To Laura, for keeping my feet on the ground, and my heart on fire—D.O.

Contents

Acknowledgments

So many individuals have contributed to this book that it boggles the mind to consider how to parcel out the thanks to each and every one. Some have been only passing acquaintances or strangers in a bar, others are longtime friends and colleagues, some others beloved managers, others less loved, and a few downright despised. As those who know us know, we tend to stick our noses into any potentially zestful interaction. Thus, it easily could be said that every chance event has added something, and so to all those with or for whom we have worked, we are grateful for the stories, ideas, simple friendship, and endurance that you have offered us. There are thanks even for those once despised (and those that we continue to scorn), for over time the positive value of even bad experience reveals itself, and sometimes even the worst has offered great value to this effort.

Specific thanks are in order, however, to many people. First, thanks to Jim Coplien and Ward Cunningham, who were initiators into the patterns community. John Vlissides is owed a debt of gratitude for his patience in reviewing our early blathering and notions and not telling us to give it up, but rather making us strive to give it something more. We are extremely grateful to Paul Taylor, down under, who spent so much of his precious time reading early versions and giving us priceless commentary that opened our eyes and our brains. Linda Rising was gracious and positive as always in her reviews, and we are thankful for her help and influence. Thanks to Mary Lynn Manns for her observations on our work and for letting us invade her groups at ChiliPLoP for our own purely selfish reasons. A tip of the hat and a deep bow to Brian Foote for his kind words and for mistaking each of our styles for the other, which gave us hope that we ultimately could blend the two.

Thanks to Dave Gerads, Tom Hull, and George Deriso for being living examples of the kinds of leaders we'd like to see cloned. A special appreciation goes to Mun Sing Lee and Monica Marics for many insightful conversations over the years about the nature of leadership. We are also grateful to Kathy Glidden for her cheerful and effective support. At Addison-Wesley, a huge thanks goes to John Fuller and Beth Burleigh Fuller for their production magic, which was flawless and beyond anything captured in a book. And to Paul Becker, our editor, we cannot convey gratitude large enough to match the risk you took in giving us this chance to publish based on our initial wild-eyed notions and semicoherent ramblings. Thank you a thousand times and a thousand times more for taking us on.

Finally, thanks to our families for putting up with it all and being the cheerleaders and sages we desperately needed so many times throughout this project. Your love and support made all the difference.

Introduction:
The Manager Pool

PATTERNS FOR RADICAL LEADERSHIP

The Manager Pool is a collection of patterns aimed at understanding and fulfilling a new vision regarding the relationship between software developers and those that lead them. This vision contains two basic elements. The first is that the effective organization radiates from a fundamental respect for individual uniqueness. The second holds that successful software development is a generative result of enlightened management, rather than a direct result of intrusive and controlling management.

The literary form known as *patterns* is used to express our observations and proves ideal for this effort, because a pattern expression implies that there are as many ways to fulfill the ideas presented within a pattern as there are readers. The use of the pattern form demands rigor in creation, yet in use it provides an inherent flexibility. Like a fluidly adaptable blueprint, its application permits software managers and developers alike to negotiate the particular reticulations of their daily work lives.

Drawn from collective experiences in the actual milieu of software development in companies both large and small, the sixty-one patterns contained in this book seek to illuminate how *people*—staff *and* management—can successfully work together to create great software products. Independent of technologies, processes, tools, or methodologies that are too often mistaken as the means of production, the fundamental conviction underlying this book is that it is always the people that matter most. As such, we hope that the patterns in the *Manager Pool* put to rest the notion that management is merely charts and graphs, technology and methodology, and instead demonstrate that to truly lead a team of talented software developers is to trust in their creative abilities and believe in their good intentions.

Have you ever noticed that software geeks love new stuff—new hardware, new operating systems, new languages, and new techniques? Mostly, though, geeks thrive on innovation—big ideas! Many not only embrace new ways of thinking, but also they often become *true believers,* exhibiting a fervor that is not so distinguishable from rabid evangelism. Although this may say nothing about the ultimate truthfulness or usefulness of a particular notion, some of these ideas do result in phenomenal breakthroughs of thought, whereas others are pathetic failures. *Patterns* is one of these potential "eurekas!" However, it remains to be seen whether this is really transcendent thinking or just another silly distraction.

With the widespread use of object-oriented technologies, the discovery and use of patterns to help build reusable software is one of the trendiest and most promising movements in software design and development. In fact, if you're reading this book, chances are you already have, or will, sign an expense voucher for *Design Patterns: Elements of Reusable Object-Oriented Software* (Gamma, Helm, Johnson, and Vlissides, Reading, MA, Addison-Wesley, 1995). Although concerned primarily with software design, in the wake of this popular book an entire patterns culture has evolved that seeks to redefine the relationships between software development, software developers, and the broader society to whom we are all ultimately obliged.

Historically, this particular concept of patterns goes back quite a bit further than 1995 and the publication of *Design Patterns,* to the effusive efforts of architect Christopher Alexander to discover and capture the qualities of those places that make people feel most alive. Although his legacy inspires from mild interest to fanaticism, his contributions are accepted universally by architects and software engineers alike for providing a common vocabulary that can be used in defining patterns.

Christopher Alexander believed that he could help people to build homes and communities that would reflect and support their lives to the utmost degree. By extracting patterns he observed in the buildings and towns of many cultures, he hoped to document those structures that ministered to our basic human and social needs and that made people feel alive. He believed that those things that fulfilled these needs were motivated by principles that could lead to tangible, objective, actionable strategies. It was his form of documenting these observations that have come to be called *patterns*.[1]

Alexander described patterns in *The Timeless Way of Building:*

> Each pattern is a three-part rule, which expresses a relation between a certain context, a problem, and a solution. . . . It is both a process and a thing; both a description of a thing which is alive, and a description of the process which will generate that thing.[2]

And from patterns, we build *pattern languages:*

> The structure of a pattern language is created by the fact that individual patterns are not isolated.[3]

In time such languages become *alive* themselves:

> Yet, changing as it is, each language is a living picture of a culture, and a way of life.[4]

In this work, the authors are concerned with improving the *human* facets of the computing experience. We believe that the use of patterns is about going beyond technique in a movement toward the essential core of successful software development—toward us, your developers. Tools don't develop software. Methodologies don't develop software. *People* develop software. And the people that develop software are not motivated in the same way as those in other aspects of the development process. The whole notion of *career* for many software developers is something completely different from what one would find among executives, marketing specialists, salespeople, or mid-level managers. A satisfied engineer may spend his or her entire career in the same nominal position, learning and creating new "stuff" for more than 25 years without a feeling of failure or regret when retirement finally comes. Would an entry-level marketing hotshot or a finance wizard with a freshly minted MBA be satisfied with a similar career trajectory? Probably not. Despite the many management gurus who believe that *motivation is motivation is motivation,*

---

1. For a more complete discussion of Software Patterns, see James O. Coplien's *Software Patterns,* SIGS Books and Multimedia, New York, 1996.
2. Alexander, C. (1979). *The Timeless Way of Building.* New York: Oxford University Press, 247.
3. Ibid., 311.
4. Ibid., 347.

regardless, we know that things are different down on the cube farm. We've lived there for a long, long time.

The authors have many years of experience in the trenches of software development and have seen a lot of trends and techniques come and go, mostly with little cumulative impact with how we ultimately do our jobs. Despite the dearth of actual improvements in how we produce software, software developers continue to see development cycles become shorter while the days get longer. The time has come to retire the old industrial models of management. The environment has become too fluid, the forms too dynamic, for us to cling tightly to old concepts, or to any concepts for that matter, that cannot flex to accommodate all the changes yet to come. *These patterns are about people working together to develop software. This book is about the relationships among these people, and, more specifically, their relationships with their leaders.*

It is in the spirit of Christopher Alexander that the authors of this book use this literary form to help technical staff and leadership better communicate within their ranks. More important, however, we hope this book will provide managers with insight into the tribe that is the development community, offering the tools they need to communicate more effectively with their development staffs.

THE PATTERNS FORM

To assist your understanding of the material, it helps to understand the form itself. With each pattern described in this book, you will often find a picture that helps set the tone or that serves as an example of what we are relating. You will find an assertion of the problem in bold type, followed by a discussion of the forces, context, and related issues. This is followed by a solution in bold type, and sometimes by our basis for making such statements. Each pattern has a name that we have carefully chosen so that it may become a *handle* for the pattern. You will discover that these handles are referenced throughout the book, creating a web by which the patterns are interrelated and rely upon each other to be perfectly fulfilled. Any time a pattern is referenced, it is referenced in capital letters in special typeface, as in FALL ON THE GRENADE, or DECIPHER DISCONTENT. Flip through the book, as necessary, to fully enjoy the patterns form. In fact, it is possible to experience the book by only reading the bolded section of the patterns as they create problem-solution pairs. When you find something particularly interesting, go back and read the entire pattern. We hope that in time you will find yourself using a kind of shorthand in your daily adventures: "He didn't survive the GAUNTLET. We might have to drop the ROTTEN FRUIT and surround the project with a CONTAINMENT BUILDING."

Our hope is that by using this form, you will be able to grasp the entire collection of these patterns as a whole, within which there are a variety of combinations in which they can be applied. Our further hope is that you will come to understand a bit more about the special nature of your software developers. Christopher Alexander wrote:

> Its result is to allow things to be alive—and this is a higher good than the victory of any one artificial system of values. The attempt to have a victory for a one-sided view of the world cannot work anyway, even for people who seem to win their point of view. The forces which are ignored do not go away just because they are ignored. They lurk, frustrated, underground. Sooner or later they erupt in violence: and the system which seems to win is then exposed to far more catastrophic dangers.[5]

As ubiquitous as software has become in our lives, while at the same time becoming increasingly invisible, the software development community has a lot to answer for and a lot to be proud of as well. It is early in our history, but that history is an accelerated one, one that will propel us beyond our ability to shape it if we do not become conscious of what we do and, more important, *why we do what we do*.

We are entering a new era, one in which work-life balance is replacing pure ambition and where the measure of personal success is not in power or money but rather in the way in which one's work supports a life. We think that this is a good thing, and we cast this modest tome into the sea in hopes that it will inspire those unknown to us to further humanize the workplace and help others to feel more alive. The generative, though perhaps seemingly indirect, effect of feeling more alive will be to produce more creatively and proficiently.

A Note on Our Particular Use of the Form

We primarily use the form as a literary device. Although it *is* fundamental that patterns be observed, we have taken the modest liberty here and there to document our collective dreams or ideas rather than hard examples in the real world. This may violate some notions in the patterns community that something should be observed in

---

5. Ibid., 304.

three separate instances, but we have not been so rigorous in all instances. If the reader prefers such rigor, then those patterns not meeting this criterion should be ignored (but read them anyway). Perhaps the dreams will be infectious.

THE VISION

Think of the traditional rural county fair, where one can watch the farm kids display the animals they have raised to be viewed; judged for excellence based on a variety of elements, such as weight, luster of coat, and overall health; and ultimately to be bought at auction. Of course, *ultimately* they are all sliced into steaks or ground into hamburger.

The Manager Pool is our hoped-for paradigm for high-tech management of the future. Today, teams do not select their managers. Projects are started under a particular manager's aegis, and then either team members are assigned to the task or the manager is granted members from the organizational pool. In some critical instances where the project is high profile or strategic, teams even may self-select the most fit members for the task. But teams never select their managers.

The pool selection process in action. This fellow was a true blue-ribbon winner.

Which begs an interesting question: In a world in which teams select their managers from a pool, would *you* be selected? Just how secure are you in your ability to lead your team into a bold new age where information technology touches all? How do the people you lead really feel about you? Do you even care? What if you stood among your peers while self-selected teams shopped for a manager? Would you be a prime pick? Or as Christopher Alexander predicts, is your system of management selection leading to catastrophic failure?

I know software developers, you may be thinking. *A bunch of whiny geeks with fat 401K plans, now dishing out advice and implying that I'm as useful as a cow.* Besides, left to their own devices, the nerds you know would choose only people who are weak or easy to manipulate to manage their teams, or who are just good-natured saps that they can push around and leave all the superfluous work to.

We admit it, this sounds amusing for a moment, but there is a more realistic point of view: *Software developers do not want weak managers.*

While the whole concept of "management" may annoy them and while they may look down upon it compared to the "purity" of software development, the geeks around you absolutely value what you do and *what you do for them.* First of all, *you* do it, not them. That's worth something. You keep the other managers off their backs, and you filter all the noise that buzzes around the project into a concise and intelligent stream. You work the interfaces and get the developers what they need so that they can focus on what it is that they do best—creating solid software. You give moral support and remind them of the value of what they do when they hit those inevitable dips and hollows. You know that if in mid-project you left, or were transferred, or promoted, that it would bring grief to your team members . . . don't you?

Corporations claim to be meritocracies, but anyone who has worked for a time in the real world knows that pure merit does not fuel a rise to the top. Ability and achievement are important, to be sure, but in a world in which the hierarchy narrows as you rise, other factors must play very large in the selection of those who are to be moved to the next rung. For many managers, unfortunately, a narrow focus upward is the nucleus of their existence. Their pains exist in pushing for success, nothing more than another appeal to those in power, and as they scratch higher, those upon whose shoulders they stand are too easily forgotten.

A manager who has the devotion of her people, we believe, will ultimately triumph over someone who plays the game only for herself. Developers don't become devoted to people who view them as interchangeable parts. If your aim is solely to ascend the corporate ladder and you are looking for a method to climb higher and faster, even if it means figuring out how to squeeze the most out of your pesky developers, then we salute your indefatigability. But we really have nothing to say that can help you. For those who are looking for a better way to be effective leaders, we vigorously salute each of you because we hope that you will become the sort of person that we would someday happily choose out of any manager pool as our leader.

The real competition is not for the attention of the executive board but for the love—yes, that's right, *love*—of your development staff, and for those in other teams who learn of your goodness by word of mouth. Think that this is some hallucinatory fantasy of ours? Well, maybe. The authors indeed have worked diligently for leaders whom they adored, and for whom they have even changed jobs and watched others change jobs for the same reason. The truly Great Ones thrive to this day, surrounded as ever by developers who have only a single condition on their employers—that they work for one of these Great Ones. Ask a few developers outright: Would they prefer to work for the slick, silver-tongued, aggressive, upwardly mobile managers down the hall, if it meant an instant 10 percent salary increase? If they would, then you have just discovered the metric for greatness (or the lack of it) in your company, although it is admittedly rather crude. If not 10 percent, then how about 15 percent? 20 percent? More? Wow! We're impressed. The more it would cost to lure your people from you, the higher you are held in their esteem.

We've been told that this idea of teams selecting managers from a pool, The Manager Pool, is a ridiculous fantasy. It smacks of social engineering, and the "powers that be" don't want to test the theory and risk complete corporate chaos. There are other well-documented and slickly presented professional programs out there that teach pleasant, risk-free approaches for accelerating production in the organization. That is, risk-free for those who think it's risky to put their own hide on the line. As for those mysterious "powers that be," we are frankly suspicious of past embraces of Total Quality Management, lifestyle policies that look good on paper, corporate reengineering, automatic code generation, and we hope that the "powers" shudder at the idea of inverting a few bricks in their hierarchical pyramid.

Our approach is rather more civilized. We are not proposing "a dialectic in the capitalist boondoggle" of software development as a secret way to topple them from their peak. *We just want the opportunity to find and work for leaders that help us to excel. And we want to excel by building software, and building it in a manner that makes the world a better place.*

This book offers you the tools to help you become the kind of manager who would be selected even in the ugliest of managerial pools by software work teams who are autonomous in the selection of their own members. We encourage you and your company to embrace the challenge and adopt The Manager Pool (or at least the attitude implicit in the concept), where leadership staff can be traded, fired from the team, or kept in perpetuity. Consider the idea of The Manager Pool as the sincerest test. You might get the Blue Ribbon.

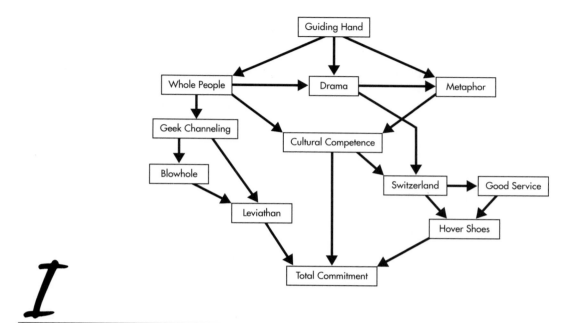

I

Psychological and Retentive Patterns

We begin our collection of patterns with those that describe more of a state of mind than a set of actions or behaviors. Attitudes form the foundation of the other patterns in this collection. These patterns are not about things that you can do, but rather about things that you understand which will inform behavior and actions, for which other patterns may apply, or for which you will have only your own good instincts to direct you.

Ned Coy, a famous Dakota cowboy, starts out for the cattle roundup with his pet "Boy Dick."

1

Guiding Hand

. . . riding a horse, running a gasoline powered, rear-tined tiller, or waxing a floor using a huge floor buffer, you might have learned that a white-knuckled grip doesn't help steer the beast where you want and exhausts you in the process. Sometimes a light touch and very little effort can drive huge forces exactly where you want them to go.

You can't control every detail, and you can't force anyone to do anything.

The most power you can bring to bear on any individual, and hence on any team, is the threat to have them fired, and that doesn't solve your problem, even if it does make you feel better for two seconds. Short of that, and we never think it's a good option unless someone is clearly destructive, you may feel the compulsion to

Photograph by John C. H. Grabill, 1888; Library of Congress, Prints & Photographs Division, John C. Grabill Collection [LC-USZ62-34595].

control things, to monitor, adjust and fine-tune at every level and opportunity. Well, forget it. You'll never find the energy, everyone will hate you for it, and you certainly won't make the Manager Pool cut. And though we can't validate this scientifically, work increases in direct proportion to the amount of meddling you do, both for you and the members of your team. If you've been running things with a death grip on every detail, we'll bet you're mighty tired, and your people are even more tired of you and your breathless panic over every little thing.

For those of you who are less extreme, you still should examine whether you are doing more than you really need to do simply to *look* like you're actively managing. Lighten your touch as an experiment, but do let your developers know that you are doing so, lest they think something's wrong. Let them do their jobs themselves and resist the urge to jump in if they neglect one of your pet project things to do. Perfect management doesn't exist when you have control of everything, but when everything that doesn't need to be managed has been left to its own nature.

> Therefore:
> Maintain a light touch, intervening here and there minimally, allowing the natural order, the geek's natural order, to move in the direction you've gently indicated. Everyone will be much less stressed, and you'll be able to spend more time cultivating your managerial wisdom.

As one of the authors was being punished by enforced managerial duties at work, it was discovered in the application of this pattern (we call this "eating our own dog food") that some staff, left to themselves, ultimately exposed their inability to self-guide or self-motivate. This discovery underscored a key point: This is not an abdication of leadership (although the author was hoping it would be), but a reminder that a "gentle guide" is still a guide. If someone on your staff still can't act, it is critical information, and the context for dealing with this individual has shifted. Find another way.

Additionally, there are times of crisis when you will have to jump up and seize the helm with great vigor and steer through some dangerous shoals to reach calmer waters. As in the use of any pattern, there is no substitute for your good judgment.

Near Checkpoint Charlie in what was formerly West Berlin, Germany.

2

Total Commitment

. . . Peter Fechter, 18 years old, to whom this memorial was erected, made a total commitment to freedom and paid for it with his life. He was allowed to bleed to death after being shot by his countrymen for trying to flee across the border.

Like many middle managers, you often feel like just one more talking head trying to figure out how to get your team to produce quickly and effectively. Furthermore, the age of the Internet has introduced unanticipated and unprecedented pressures to deliver complex software at blinding rates, even in large and profitable companies. Your company relies on you to turn out software that will prove your company can cut the mustard in a world of time-to-market races that bend the time-space continuum. Customers are smart, stockholders are skittish, and your competition is one click away. Your company will either produce good software or close up shop.

◆◆◆

Not only are the expectations of your bosses and the associated pressures hard to live with, you hoped that your life would amount to more than cracking the project schedule whip in the air. It seems almost impossible to lead your team to successfully implement against insane software deliverable schedules without them growing to abhor your very presence.

Perhaps you are a person with the unfulfilled notion that an accomplished life is more than just personal achievement and wealth, but a willingness and commitment to making a positive impact on the people that you work with and ask so much of. It may be that you are already halfway down that cold stone path of animosity with your developers. Your developers are distant and positively glacial in their interactions with you. You suspect that not only do they harbor a real distaste for you, but that you're the butt of their jokes. Because you haven't programmed since Fortran77 was popular, you have no idea whether your programmers are even producing to their potential or building products of any quality. Because you are essentially a nontechnical person these days, your developers can tell you anything and you have to believe what they tell you—you want to believe. You don't understand their TRIBAL LANGUAGE(17). Basically, you're wedged hard between the trite and the cliché—you want to succeed as a manager, but you are nothing without your developers.

We're in a talent shortage here. Even after the dotCrash dominated the news in the year 2000 and reliable companies are weakening fixed-income retirement plans, those with true talent are not worried. There is no looking back from the age of technocracy. High-tech employees have no need or reason to be loyal to you or to your company. If you can find the strength to become their weapon against the idiocies they perceive, and bludgeon, stab, or explode the insane ideas about schedules and costs that emanate from above, then you will hold the power. To lead, you must know yourself as more than a functionary.

While some may rightly argue the fad-like nature of the *Cluetrain Manifesto*[1] we giggle aloud at the following commentary, ". . . we don't care about business—per se, per diem, au gratin. . . . Cost of sales and bottom lines and profit margins—if

---

1. Levine, Rick, Christopher Locke, Doc Searls, and David Weinberger (2000). *The Cluetrain Manifesto.* Cambridge, MA: Perseus Books, 182.

you're a company, that's your problem. But if you *think* of yourself as a company, you've got much bigger worries. We strongly suggest you repeat the following mantra as often as possible until you feel better: 'I am not a company. I am a human being.'"[2] And developers, however cynical, vain, self-absorbed, and unknowing as they may seem, do have an absolute adoration for someone who can and will defy upper-management when it is called for. You become a combination sage and savior to them. They will know that you understand them, that their cause is your cause, and that you will shield them from harm and serve them with support.

And they will reward you with good software, delivered on time.

A snapshot of the desired relationship
between management and developers
in spirit, if not in fact.

Whatever loyalty they are capable of having will be loyalty to you. Remember that they can survive without you. In fact, a manager's slow, painful demise can be quite entertaining. But a good manager is a rare and precious thing. Think about it:

---

2. Ibid.

You, alone, out in the marketplace competing against all the other middle managers—how do you prove your worth over another? It's a gloomy reality for a legion of managers who have been "released" or "reallocated" by their major global companies. When you have a legion of developers willing to follow you to a new company in an economy that is critically short of such skills, you become the goose that can lay the golden egg. Their collective curriculum vitae is your calling card.

Lest you imagine that we are rubbing our hands together in gleeful anticipation that you might actually believe what we are saying and destroy yourself in the process, give it your own litmus test. Put your loafers up on your L-shaped, ergonomically correct, faux-oak desk and think about some of the best managers you know—managers who seem to have a rapport with their developers. Now ask: How many of those developers did they work with at a previous company? How many came along with them when the manager switched jobs? In fact, some of the great technical talents bring their managers with *them*.

Understand, however, that *commitment* to succeed alone is not enough. Some of the most committed leaders throughout the history of the world were horrible destructive forces—Hitler, Stalin, Pinochet. If you follow in their footsteps, then your level of commitment will be admirable (risking total global destruction or the annihilation of various ethnos is pretty heavy), but it is clearly misguided at best and psychotically, horribly, unimaginably wrong at worst. Beyond commitment, it is critical to exercise ethical discretion. Remember this if nothing else: *There is never a substitute for honest, human judgment.*

You will never, ever be able to reduce the management of human beings engaged in creative endeavor to a series of homilies or a top-ten list of things to do. Even this book should be suspect. Context must always inform your decisions, and no boilerplate techniques will always be applicable. That's a good thing, of course. If management was reducible to such simplistic formulae, then you yourself would be automated out of existence. Our thinking is directly contrary to that of the management guru W. Edwards Deming who might have said, "What can't be measured can't be managed"; we say, "What can't be measured *must* be managed." Count as a blessing the complexity of life.

Fight the urge to side with your bosses (be they human or in spreadsheet form) against the concerns and interests of your team. If you discover that you are just some sort of a dumb pipe between the wishes of *your* leadership and the work that is required of your developers, you are nothing more than a lackey. If you just try to clean up the messes left behind by your developers to make them somehow excusable to your management, then you are nothing more than an overpaid domestic employee swinging around a toilet brush. Chances are—if you're like many of the alleged leaders we've worked for—you are all of the above. But maybe it's time to be more. We're not asking you to defy the gunners in the tower and the land mines across No Man's Land, but we are asking you to make a break for the other side and take some risk in letting both sides see where you are headed. Do it with TOTAL COMMITMENT.

Strive to become a true leader, not a prepackaged, off the shelf, "I read the *dummies* book" leader, or the sociopathic leader who is convinced of her profound skills by virtue of her bank account or fancy new truck. Leadership doesn't come from a seminar or the shelf at your favorite chain bookstore, nor is it measured in dollars and cents; it comes from working on behalf of your team and acting with a clear head in regard to the larger business goals. Learn to realize that people really are the means of production and that your success depends on your team respecting you for your defense of them from the machinations of outside forces.

Speaking truth to power may seem like a career-limiting, pension-forgoing move, but it is indeed the reverse. When you have a team that respects you and likes working for you, then wherever you go, many will follow. Leave the psychological chains of your financial lock-up behind.

You will hold the power.

Therefore:
Commit to discovering and understanding the nature of your team as individuals who are destined to carry forth the ethos of their tribe. Discover what truly motivates them. Dig deep to find the courage to act on what you know and learn about them. Speak their truth to your bosses. Risk intelligent martyrdom for your people.

Of course, it's easy or fun to ask someone to risk martyrdom and the bread for their table, but we aren't really asking you to pour gasoline on your head and light a match. We want you to act courageously, even when there is personal risk involved. Yes, you may lose your job; yes, your team may wave good-bye to you at the electronically monitored, card-key-controlled door, but at least you'll have your conscience. Is it enough?

One aspect of a great whale while the entirety retains its wonderful mystery.

3

Leviathan

. . . software projects are huge beasts, difficult to grasp in their entirety, given the fluid environment in which they swim: changing requirements, drifting priorities, unexpected business disturbances, and unmapped technical shoals.

Software systems of any real utility are impossible to see in their entirety. Their understanding is bound up in the humans who create. In a human enterprise, not every nuance can be documented and understood. But without good documentation, you know that you will suffer undue losses if you lose staff or you must validate the value of your technology.

Many good engineers—clever designers, solid developers—don't document things that your company's standards might require be documented. When they do

---

document, they don't maintain the documentation when a last minute change, bug fix, or feature is plugged in. There's never enough time in the breakneck schedules to update code, user documentation, system documentation, and everything else that shudders up from below. All software developers understand this, so when they are faced with learning a new system and fixing it, they are more likely to turn directly to the code than to consult some likely worthless document.

Over time, the software system can begin to take on the form of Herman Melville's well-known whale, lurking just beneath the surface of the sea:

> The living whale, in his full majesty and significance, is only to be seen at sea in unfathomable waters; and afloat the vast bulk of him is out of sight, like a launched line-of-battle ship; and out of that element it is a thing eternally impossible for mortal man to hoist him bodily in the air, so as to preserve all his mighty swells and undulations. . . . For all these reasons then, any way you look at it, you must needs[1] conclude that the great Leviathan is that one creature in the world which must remain unpainted to the last. True, one portrait may hit the mark nearer than another, but none can hit it with any very considerable degree of exactness. So there is no earthly way of finding out precisely what the whale really looks like.[2]

In the software project that is your LEVIATHAN, the beast can turn in another direction at a moment's notice. If anyone leaves, some indispensable knowledge may leave with him or her. Above all else, software systems of any consequence are often too large and too integrated in their environment to be hoisted clear so that one can grasp them in their entirety and detail simultaneously and then deploy personnel and resources most effectively. Even if the great beast *could* be hoisted clear and then lain out for autopsy and cataloging of each part and its relationship to the whole, what you would know would be static, and soon useless. Think of the countless postmortem analyses that have been done of past projects. Whatever became of those documents and reports? Were they studied and discussed and factored into the next planning cycle or held in hand as another team was assembled and dispatched to hunt the behemoth? Probably not, if our experience is any indication; and even if they were examined closely for clues as to the conduct of the next expedition, they would reveal scant hard information to apply.

---

1. Yes, this *is* an archaic form, but after reading Melville, it just sounds so much more compelling.
2. Melville, Herman (1983). *Moby Dick*. New York: Literary Classics of the United States, 1076.

Even worse, in addition to being large and incomprehensible as a whole, software projects are complex and often chaotic. Our natural tendency is try and control whatever we can to reduce uncertainty, but any manager with real experience knows that controlling the LEVIATHAN is not only exceedingly difficult, it's pointless. David Whyte noted in his book about work, *The Heart Aroused,* that:

> A manager *manages,* but only a human soul gifted with imagination has the resilient artistry to live and work with forces that call for deeper strategies than containment.[3]

This state of things, however unnerving to the ideal of managerial control, is actually a liberating condition. In first admitting one's powerlessness, one becomes free to observe and to reflect without the constant imperative to act. By signing on to lead teams through projects, you expose yourself to these raw elements, but it is the only way to learn again. Melville, again:

> And the only mode in which you can derive even a tolerable idea of his living contour, is by going whaling yourself; but by so doing, you run no small risk of being eternally stove and sunk by him. Wherefore, it seems to me you had best not be too fastidious in your curiosity touching this Leviathan.[4]

In going after the software project, you must accept the nature of the beast: large, shape-shifting, complex, and dangerous. You cannot control or even contain the monster, but you are not powerless. The vastness that might overpower you and the chaos that may undermine you have principles of self-organization that, if recognized and permitted to occur, can aid you. David Whyte, discussing *strange attractors,* notes this phenomenon:

> Firstly, and most useful, the image of the strange attractor tells us that even the most entangled and chaotic of systems is made up of many orderly behaviors; it's just that none of them can ultimately dominate the larger pattern, but scientists have found that if the system is disturbed in certain ways, one of those many regular behaviors can be encouraged to emerge. Built into a chaotic system, then, is an unusual flexibility that

---

3. Whyte, David (1994). *The Heart Aroused: Poetry and the Preservation of the Soul in Corporate America.* New York: Currency-Doubleday, 220.
4. Melville, Herman (1983). *Moby Dick.* New York: Literary Classics of the United States, 1076–1077.

allows it to switch quickly between many different behaviors, making it inherently adaptable and multifaceted.[5]

We meet the LEVIATHAN much as the whalers in the nineteenth century did—at the edge where two worlds meet. For the whalers it was where the sea met the sky; for you, it is chaos and order. You must tread this interface deftly, subtly initiating a GUIDING HAND (1) here, consciously avoiding intervention there. Do not dive below and try to understand the behemoth in its own environment, nor ascend to your own aerie, to observe but not participate.

Therefore:
Apply effort in guiding those areas that are regular and understood by you and your team. Document those in a manner to satisfy the fundamental requirement of the organization to have an understanding of its systems. Avoid meddling in the gray, submerged technical areas that you do not or cannot fully understand. Accept that beauty exists in this marvelous beast as it moves in its mysterious ways. Trust in the natural forces at work, and in your developers in their labors, to arrange themselves with only your gentle intervention.

5. Whyte, David (1994). *The Heart Aroused: Poetry and the Preservation of the Soul in Corporate America.* New York, Currency-Doubleday, 246–247.

Carol Stimmel in a dramatic moment? From the Musée Rodin, Paris, France.

Drama

. . . work occupies more of our continuous waking hours than any of our other activities. In the drama of our lives it is a large part of the plot, frequently taking center stage. We shape the rest of our lives around work: where we live, when we play, when we take vacations, even how we raise our children (e.g., Don't talk to me, I had a bad day at work!*). Yet it seems that the idea of life as drama, that our lives are composed of stories, is a very unknown tool for working with other human beings and creating or understanding specific cultures.*

A sense of drama can greatly motivate a team, and your role as a manager demands that you, at the very least, set the stage and define the possible outcomes. However much of the developers' working hours are, if not exactly drudgery, commonplace, they still wish to be a part of the story.

Developers, although they would deny it if asked directly, want desperately to be in and of the story, the drama of success and failure. All of us love to tell stories, and not surprisingly, the source of our favorite stories is our own lives. When David Whyte, in *The Heart Aroused,* claimed that "Work is drama, and our inability to live vitally on its stage has much to do with the modern loss of dramatic sensibility, the lost sense that we play out our lives as part of a greater story . . . ,"[1] he was describing the absolute need for drama and myth as the sustenance that will help us drag through our daily labors.

Face it, as a manager, you probably tell lots of stories (to clients especially). But, in this case, we're not talking about the fables you tell just to survive the next executive weekly review meeting. We're talking about the ability to frame and set the story of the voyage—what dangers lurk, what rewards may be reaped. To lead your team into a project with a sense of drama, of good and evil in the collective endeavor, and stories of heroes who have come before is *essential* and *necessary.*

Does this sound wacky, far-out, and too weird even for this book? Good. This is exactly what is needed in these days of lost corporate loyalty, distrust, and allegiance only to self. You can no longer sincerely offer security, certain riches, comfort, or safety; and besides, none of that really has a chance to make history. In fact, one could argue that the clamor for security in work is sprung from a corresponding loss of drama and integration of work with the lives of workers. "If I am to be bored to death in these endeavors, at least compensate me in some manner that wasting my years won't seem so stupid." Look, everyone wants to make a mark in life, and you have the opportunity and responsibility to help define that mark! If you don't somehow distinguish the work, they simply will not believe in the necessity of the project at hand.

When you tell them you have a vision, they hope for a real mission, a real comprehension of the issues at hand. Sadly, the pabulum that gets spooned out is a pile of equivocation and doublespeak:

> Our vision at Blowhard, as the preeminent software development powerhouse, is to enable our customers to benefit from the most cutting-edge, quantum-leaping solutions for their mission-critical applications. We at Blowhard strive to delight our customers by delivering best-of-breed enterprisewide solutions for the complex age of eCommerce, always

---

1. Whyte, David (1994). *The Heart Aroused: Poetry and the Preservation of the Soul in Corporate America.* New York, Currency-Doubleday, 18–19.

exceeding the client's expectations. And, in addition, we strive to have work-life balance.

Just for the sake of comparison, consider the vision statement of Mother Jones, an 82-year-old labor leader, speaking to militant coal miners on the steps of the West Virginia Capitol, July 22, 1905:

> It is freedom or death, and your children will be free. We are not going to leave a slave class to the coming generation, and I want to say to you that the next generation will not charge us for what we've done; they will charge and condemn us for what we have left undone.

When the chill you have subsides, take a moment to consider the difference in impact, the stage that each vision sets. Then, decide.

Inspiring software developers to do the job you have hired them to do may not be as rousing as ending child labor for all time, but the software that sends a rocket to space and brings the astronauts back safely is pretty important. We would rather hear a rousing speech than the mealymouthed horse hockey that is as inspiring as watching the water circle down into the toilet bowl. Not only are statements of broad corporate vision spiritless, but companies often fail in the commitment to really follow through on their words. "If we are such a powerhouse, why can't I double the memory on my development box so I don't spend half the day hearing my hard drive thrash?" And, most unfortunately, in the wake of every new vision statement comes a person who is even more cynical and stigmatized by perfunctory, limp, and insincere gestures dreamed up by functionaries far removed from the front lines of development.

Constantin Stanislavsky understood how to make the elements of drama work, how to make it real and natural. He laid the foundation for generations to come on the American stage and in film by paring away theatricality and perfunctory gesture. Consider his instruction from the viewpoint of project as plot and you as actor:

> In a play, the whole stream of individual, minor objectives, all the imaginative thoughts, feelings, and actions of an actor, should converge to carry out the *super-objective* of the plot. The common bond must be so strong that even the most insignificant detail, if it is not related to the *super-objective,* will stand out as superfluous or wrong.[2]

2. Stanislavsky, Constantin (1948). *An Actor Prepares.* New York: Theatre Arts, 256.

You, as the manager, must be constantly vigilant that activities that do not *directly* serve your goals do not creep in to sap the creative energy and belief of your developers. If you have your developers draw up plans and strategies and collect metrics because that is "how it is done" at your company, and not because they will have a direct and beneficial effect on the outcome of your project, then you are throwing in false gestures and phony emotion in the hope of fooling your audience. Such hollow efforts won't stave off failure and may actually contribute to project demise by sapping the reality of your project drama and injuring the belief of your developers in the project. If, however, you do your job and ensure that each activity is value added to your objective, it will help further to power your team. Stanislavsky again:

> If it is human and directed toward the accomplishment of the basic purpose of the play, it will be like a main artery, providing nourishment and life to both it and the actors.[3]

When developers see that everything they are asked to do has a sound reason, and when they see that you are an active gatekeeper, it is far more likely that they will remain inspired and nourished by your project goals.

Therefore:
To accomplish your goals, you need developers who, while at work, live *vitally* upon the stage of your project. You desperately need an alignment between their internal motivation and the greater purpose of the project, and this greater purpose has to be articulated *by you.* Your team must be both inspired and locked into a common understanding of the *super-objective.* Every duty that arises must be inextricably bound to the purposes of your super-objective: delivery on your commitments.

DRAMA(4) is closely related to the use of METAPHOR(5) and sets the stage for successfully incorporating patterns into your everyday management strategies, such as OUTCOME BASED(20), TOTAL COMMITMENT(2), and most of the project management patterns included in this book.

---

3. Ibid.

Statue of Freedom, though not freedom itself.

5

Metaphor

. . . humans are, by nature, storytellers and listeners. The narrative form helps give meaning to the world and the time through which it moves. It frames and shapes events so that we can connect them, adding rhythms and flows. Narrative works to help memory in this way, but it also helps us to comprehend the larger questions and to recognize the larger forces and patterns that rule life.

If someone were to ask you what stories informed your style of management, what would you say? Do you have a story that articulates your journey, or have you come from nothing at all? Do you find it difficult to connect powerfully with the desires of your developers?

Photograph by Theodor Horydczak, taken sometime between 1920 and 1950. Library of Congress, Prints & Photographs Division, Theodor Horydczak Collection [LC-H834-S07-060 DLC].

Does this frighten you to consider, or does it make no sense? If it frightens you, is it because you suddenly sense an abyss opening up for which you have no comprehension? Or is it simply that you may be starting to think that you have wasted your money on a book such as this which contains odd and rather difficult questions? What about those simplistic formulae and happy similes you have grown to count on in your management books?

We are asking you to consider something more, and perhaps a bit bizarre— that there is a structure to the pattern of events that led you to this point. Understanding the stories and metaphors that define who you are today will provide the framework you need to become the kind of leader you want to be.

What inspires you to lead? What made you want to become a leader in the first place? Is this a difficult thing to explain? What was the story from somewhere in your earlier years that caught you and held you and somehow led you to this point in your life? Or were you just accidentally pushed into this position to fill a gap in the organizational chart, and you've experienced vertigo ever since the day you were promoted?

Here are some stories to consider: Was your father a barbarian against whom you were defenseless, leading you to ruthlessly claw to a position of power? Did you have an English teacher who was able to inspire even the most unlikely of students, like you, with her creative leadership? Was your mother a jackbooted fascist, who slapped you down on a cold toilet seat the day you were two? Do you see her face when your supervisor asks for your weekly status report? Was your favorite camp counselor a really great listener, making you feel at the top of the world? Perhaps you could choose from one of these.

If you are now completely lost and irritated, please understand that you are not alone. In our experience, realizing you have no stories that frame your present reality is so common that it leads us to think that much of the leadership, or what passes for it in the software world, is largely unconscious. *Unconscious!* We sometimes wonder whether large numbers of somnambulists aren't working software developers to death. If a leader does not know why she does what she does, nor regularly questions what drives the collective decisions made and paths blazed, how is this different from sleepwalking and hoping to wake up before you wander onto the interstate highway? Traveling on autopilot makes sense when cruising at 23,000 feet, but it is not recommended when the margin for error is small.

A short example in storytelling in the professional world might help. We know a manager who asked all of her interview candidates to tell a story about themselves:

"What was your first job, and what lesson did you learn from it?" Some were stumped, and they simply weren't hired. Others told tales of fast food and secretarial nightmares. One candidate reminisced about a project where she needed to stuff 100 flyers into 100 preaddressed envelopes. Her boss had given her a sheet of instructions, but they were tossed aside for such a stupid, simple task. For God's sake, she was smart enough to stuff envelopes! When she was almost done, she noticed that the flyers had people's names on them and were supposed to go into the appropriately addressed envelope. She carefully had to unglue, restuff, and reglue all the envelopes back together again. What did she learn? To read the manual (or, using TRIBAL LANGUAGE(17), "RTFM it!").

People need a greater purpose overarching their efforts if they are to succeed on a regular basis. Metaphors, stories, and folktales provide the cognitive connection that ultimately binds us together. If we listen to each other's stories, we can move one step closer to authentic understanding (see CULTURAL COMPETENCE(9)). Articulating this on a personal level particularly for leaders is crucial, but it is also necessary for everyone working on a project.

Metaphor and storytelling glue an organization together, not with doctrine or lists of commandments as described in DRAMA(4), but with an understanding of the common rhythms and flows that project life takes.

Therefore:
Discover the metaphors, stories, and folktales that inspire you to lead. Think about them and take time to articulate them. They will inform, motivate, and guide you toward understanding how and why you are a leader. Encourage your team to spin yarns about their lives and how they ended up in jobs where they gleefully hack code until midnight. If you haven't quit your job by the end of this exercise, then perhaps you are in the right place after all; otherwise—congratulations!

The use of METAPHOR has its place in the use of many of the patterns defined in this book, most especially in seeing your team members as WHOLE PEOPLE(8). It will also lead you to a greater level of comfort with the application of other patterns, such as SHAMELESS IGNORAMUS(14), EXHIBITIONISM(13), and TOTAL COMMITMENT(2). Through the use of metaphor and storytelling you will become more comfortable with the individual members of your team.

The mountains as shields of neutrality.

6

Switzerland

. . . managers are often forced into positions where they must side with one entity or another in their organization. This phenomenon operates at many levels, from the systemic to the deeply personal, and seems to be one of the basic requirements for maintaining power.

Your senior leadership may encourage rivalry and struggle among managers as a method of systematizing power agency in their organization. But, taking part in the struggle of colleagues is a dangerous game and one that can cause you to abandon yourself in the process.

Much like the playground manipulators of our long-gone childhood, companies may encourage your participation in conflicts of many types. For example, the

Matterhorn, between 1880 and 1910, photographer unknown. Library of Congress, Prints and Photographs Division, Detroit Publishing Company Collection [LC-D428-45038 DLC].

backing of a particular political candidate because of the candidate's stand on certain issues concerning business or regulation, the filling out of forms that let you anonymously rate the behavior of your peers (usually as a way of maneuvering them out of a job), and the insidious use of one manager's success against another. It may also manifest itself more uncomfortably in the context of a close colleague who feels he is being stabbed in the back by your mutual boss and is trying desperately to gain your allegiance.

The temptation to pick a side is probably born of your desire to experience DRAMA(4) in life, especially when your days are filled with signing expense vouchers and listening to your managing vice president's latest clueless idea. Trying to look interested or reiterating why it's a bad idea to develop an interactive interface that lets customers change TV channels via telephone can leave one desensitized, to say the least. But you don't want to be the perfect stooge for carrying out major acts of intrigue that can lead directly to personal disaster.

We think there is a better, alternative approach; stay out of it. In fact, the country of Switzerland has been quite successful with its model of neutrality. It is theorized that as early as the fifteenth century Switzerland swore off cases of conflict between disputing parties. Even when in the middle of a war zone, the Swiss have managed to convince the world of the validity of their neutrality and thus compelled the warring nations to respect its boundaries. In the age of globalization, how has such a small country managed to protect itself from the temptations of global politics?

In an interesting twist, neutral Switzerland still maintains an army. While the country constitutionally chooses to remain neutral in perpetuity, the country finds that because it may not align itself with any other nation either offensively or defensively, it must be prepared to defend itself against aggression from all to guarantee its neutral status. Contrary to any other notion, Switzerland isn't just a bird on a wire waiting to get popped—it is an *active* nonparticipant. Naturally, its geography is a great help. Were it as flat as Poland and situated between great hostile empires, neutrality would hardly be a reasonable option. Keep that in mind in your political dealings, and understand that when you have the power of your developers at your beck and call (TOTAL COMMITMENT(2)) and when you are central in a large-scale effort (LEVIATHAN(3)), you have both the army and terrain to become as Switzerland.

One must wonder, of course, if the position of neutrality and the ability to continue economic relations with both sides in a warring conflict have allowed the Swiss to bask in the glow of perpetual self-interest without responsibility. It can be argued that it is the outright rejection of any involvement in conflict that allows Switzerland to execute protective missions such as those associated with disaster aid or the granting of asylum. Whatever your political thinking in this matter, the Swiss have managed to maintain their borders for hundreds of years.

For the manager in the quick-shifting world of high technology, taking a neutral position can be difficult, especially when what defines corporate direction is defined by whoever is left standing after marathon strategy meetings. Taking the example of Switzerland, it may be easier to envision how a position of personal neutrality in the face of brutal politics allows the forward-thinking manager to emerge unscathed. Unlike the powerful managers and leaders in your company who will use force the moment their needs aren't met, the neutral manager resists the desire to exercise shameless acts of power, confident in her ability to defend herself at a moment's notice.

This is an exceedingly rare trait in a leader. One multimedia developer we know worked in a broadcasting station that provided a traditional FM-band broadcast as well as streaming feeds of news and music shows for global Internet listeners. The stress was high at this operation, because live feeds had to be pulled off the satellite without mishap at all hours of the day and news stories were produced under fire, and all had to be encoded for real-time and archived for immediate just-in-time delivery to a global audience.

Factions were rife in this business. When deadlines were blown and feeds garbled, and when employees were scrambling for a fall guy, one particular manager seemed to consistently rise above the fray. Mike Redding (name changed) was the news manager, and news was the central hub of activity. He was in the perfect position to take it all in the chest whenever things went wrong. But his day-to-day languorous attitude allowed him to continue managing his news team without distraction. Every crisis seemed to pass him by, and his yearly physicals were just fine.

A vivid example includes an early event that occurred with the organization about the time he came to work there—cries of racial discrimination countered by anti-Semitism broke out and rose all the way to the level of legal scrutiny, yet he never even once gave his opinion of the matter. And while the struggle went on for more than a year, causing intermittent hallway screaming sessions, swastikas placed strategically around the company, and untold dollars in psychotherapy, he never said more than to lament the strife among his colleagues. Ultimately, he could work with whoever came out on top, by keeping cordial relationships with all parties involved throughout.

He never repeated gossip, and when gossip was repeated to him, he wouldn't make eye contact with the talker or acknowledge the gossip with more than a non-committal, absent-sounding *hmmm*. He wouldn't ask clarifying questions or try to parse out who was wrong and wronged. Not only was it boring to try to drag Mike into the fray, one often felt a little dirty and shamed after making the attempt. No one complained that he didn't get involved; more often the comment was heard about how great and fair he was. Most amazingly, you couldn't get him to give up his neutrality even with the most clever word games and flowing beer. The man was solid in his investment of a neutral position toward political dogfights, no matter how enraged the embattled became. Mike lived out the admonition in the revered *I Ching*, "You will be blameless if you are impartial to others."

> Therefore:
> Treat outside conflict and whispered rumors with a position of neutrality that acknowledges that many of the political battles and wars raging around will ultimately have no impact on the greater good of the organization, your group, and your team. The point is not to dodge responsibility, but to survive the political divisions and consolidations raging around you. A leader must convincingly portray her neutrality by showing complete disinterest in the politics of the organization, never engaging in gossip, and never being an eager recipient of the latest juicy news.

There may be times when it is incumbent upon you morally to provide GOOD SERVICE(7), but this is not in conflict with an experienced position of neutrality if practiced judiciously. Again, let context and your own good judgment inform your choices.

Diner. Clinton, Indiana, 1940.

7

Good Service

. . . some eating establishments make it a daily part of doing business to offer their local civil servants a cup of coffee or nosh on the house. They hope that when they are in need that their kind acts will somehow be remembered.

Through the use of SWITZERLAND(6)-style neutrality we observed how it is possible to survive political division in your company. Neutrality is difficult because it is human nature to be involved with the personal lives of others. In fact, it comprises one of the most fundamental aspects of being human.

Sometimes acts of political aggression in the corporate environment can be so reprehensible that it seems equally corrupt not to step in to attempt to stop the behavior. Yet to do so could be destructive to your managerial status and could violate your self-imposed neutrality toward getting involved with objectionable events that do not directly affect you.

Most of us have seen it before. The manager dresses down the abject developer who made an error in her code and checked it back in, thereby breaking the entire build and shutting down the development process until the error was repaired. Or the leader accuses a hapless meeting attendee of a lack of creativity when a problem was reported. We were just glad it wasn't us that time, because sooner or later, for any developer working long hours and cranking out complicated code parcels daily, mistakes simply are made and propagated. It's the nature of something as deep and strange as any LEVIATHAN(3). Yes, most developers who have been around long enough have seen people manipulated, cursed at, and victimized by false vision and promise. What we really are wondering is why and how these managers, these leaders, ever found their way into a position of authority; and furthermore, why these managers find it incumbent upon their positions to degrade and humiliate their own team members. These are the very people upon whom they must rely for their personal success in this business (see WHOLE PEOPLE(8)).

Overlooked and tacitly accepted acts of degradation toward other people are harmful to the victims and are a systemic virus in your corporation that will ultimately affect everyone. Not only is it extremely disheartening to believe that one must run down others to prove one's worth, it is equally damaging to the soul (whatever you believe that may be) to turn a blind eye toward the debasing acts of one's peers in the workplace. A Protestant pastor and early supporter of the Nazis, Martin Niemoller, lamented his inability to speak up early in the face of oppression in this well-known poem:

> *First they came for the Communists,*
> *and I didn't speak up,*
> *because I wasn't a Communist.*
> *Then they came for the Jews,*
> *and I didn't speak up,*
> *because I wasn't a Jew.*
> *Then they came for the Catholics,*
> *and I didn't speak up,*
> *because I was a Protestant.*
> *Then they came for me,*

*and by that time there was no one
left to speak up for me.*

Although Niemoller narrowly escaped his own execution at Dachau, his poem exposed the ultimate effects of complicity in allowing the suffering of others. Gratefully, you will not often find murder in the workplace of today, but you can easily find both subtle and overt acts of cruelty, rudeness, and debasement. Although some managers are overtly unkind and severe with their teams, many managers tend to disguise their sadistic tendencies in a neatly wrapped package that they call "being a straight shooter." The translation: I shoot people down the minute they speak up. You can recognize these leaders because, despite their attempts to *involve* their team members in discussions or to *encourage* dialogue and questions, the room is very quiet. When the lone questioner pipes up, the leader who answers curtly in a tone that drips with the implication that that question was one of the stupidest questions ever asked can easily discourage questions from other team members. Or, more subtly, the manager who always comments, "Well, that's a good idea, but *if you fail . . . ,*" soon discourages risk and creativity.

That's just style! you may object, and perhaps, in all fairness, it often is. Some leaders simply don't know how to effectively lead and take pride in their lack of temper; some are threatened by confrontation; others are socially inept; and still others just want to keep it easy because they, too, are frustrated and tired. Yet it is these subtle acts that you yourself may depend on when management-by-desperation creeps into your day. Such subtlety is nearly impossible to confront. Often, the developers on the team really have nothing to pin their discomfort on; they just feel a creeping sense of worthlessness and depression. They usually will quit, be reassigned, or find some other way to avoid the malfeasance of their leaders. One engineer we know, who tends toward these kinds of managers, said, "It's like I'm repeatedly being drafted by the Tampa Bay Buccaneers!" (one of the worst National Football League teams). Her managers tend toward professional slights, sarcasm, and outrageous statements that they would posit if only to negate her. After leaving the company, she still has instantaneous contrary reactions to people who display the same, rather common, physical and social characteristics of these individuals, and she still feels jittery around managers who might be suspected of the desire to negate her efforts.

Of course, if the reprehensible one is your own manager, or another higher authority in the company, your problem may be more complicated. It seems rather foolish to walk into the managing vice president's office and tell him that he's alienating his staff with his rude behavior. You might be accused of weakness or trying to create a hole in the hierarchy that you dream to fill. A wise manager has to carefully pick a way through that one, but we believe that it is much more harmful to the organization and its members to allow a sore like that to fester. You can bet that if you've observed this kind of behavior on a chronic basis that many people have been directly affected by it and have either left the company altogether or found a way to avoid it. We're not talking about the occasional grumps or the ill-timed surge of managerial testosterone or even the use of DIRECT ACTION(19) that leaves some feeling stung.

We are talking about the powerful among you who use degradation, no matter how abstruse, as a means for a managerial end.

> Therefore:
> When you witness behavior from anyone at any time that is degrading to another, you are morally compelled to address it. Approach the offender quietly and personally, if appropriate, and explain why his actions are unacceptable. Suggest more effective ways to handle frustration. In extreme cases, step in and instigate official action.

This is one of the foundation patterns for The Manager Pool. It is elemental to treating others as WHOLE PEOPLE(8) and leading with a sense of TOTAL COMMITMENT(2). Although we cannot ignore the possible unpleasantness and negative consequences in the short-term for inserting yourself into such situations, the long-term effects for intervening will be worth it. Asserting the moral high ground is not a walk in the park; rather, it is a difficult climb. That's why there is so little company up there when you achieve it.

June in January, Miami Beach, Florida, 1939.

8

Whole People

. . . people often have lives that extend beyond the office.

A software development team, however assembled and assigned to a project, consists of individuals, many (not all, we've noticed) of whom have lives quite apart from their work. As part of a team, each shows one dimension, and for the technical skills of each as an individual, a second dimension is revealed. To appear in depth, however, a third dimension is essential, and its aspect resides in life beyond the team and the project.

Understanding what makes each individual tick, apart from the team and apart from the technology, is the key to motivating individuals. Furthermore, developers are more likely to respond with enthusiasm when your calls for their additional help are framed in the understanding of their greater lives.

Photograph by Marion Post Wolcott, 1939; Library of Congress, Prints & Photographs Division, FSA-OWI Collection [LC-USF33-030468-M4 DLC].

31

Sincerity is a continuous process, and it does not serve you if your concern for their home life crops up only whenever you ask them for yet more overtime.

While watching software developers wandering around in tribes, babbling in their often incomprehensible TRIBAL LANGUAGE(17) as they chug high-caffeine beverages, it is difficult to imagine them as musicians, carpenters, actors, parents, or fly fishermen. In fact, for many managers, thinking of their team in this way interferes with their ability to ask their teams to work yet another 70 hours for the sake of the project. Too often, the grueling hours are spent in dehumanizing cubes (see the related patterns LIVING SPACE(53), PUBLIC SPACE(57), and PRIVATE SPACE(56)), solving arcane problems, under great pressure from management and peers alike. Adding insult to injury, often such sacrifice is dedicated to building ill-conceived or incompetently marketed applications, or on projects that will most certainly fail due to some ineptitude in scheduling, staffing, or budgeting. Knowing that people may be giving up a holiday with their children, or a long-planned vacation with their loved ones, when you have knowledge that the project is likely to be canceled any day now or will wither eventually can be hard to live with (or should be, anyway), even for the manager who sneaks peeks at Machiavelli's *The Prince*.

If ever your ambition for success has blinded you to the pain and sacrifice that constant overtime can create in people's lives, now is the time to stop looking at them as *resources* and look at them as complete *human beings*. While the board or the executive committee may see them only as staff numbers or corporate assets, you are obligated to make the conversion from staffing chart heads to human faces. It is your noble mission to understand these individuals and learn what makes them want to get up in the morning. Maybe such a mission could lead you to spearhead a regimen of OVERTIME DETOX(23) someday.

There are thousands of feel-good books on the market that hinge on establishing that magic balance between our life and our work. Although those books are fabulous to read while sipping a Mai Tai with your toes dipped in the pool, they lack context and understanding for the realities of the modern-day software development environment. We have seen much worse befall our colleagues than a life out of balance. We have seen (and yes, sometimes become) people who seem to have lost their entire spirit in the pursuit of the relentless problems that software development presents. We prefer Joseph Campbell in the *Power of Myth*[1] as our manage-

---

1. Campbell, Joseph (1988). *The Power of Myth*. New York: Doubleday, 3.

ment guru, "When you get to be older, and the concerns of the day have all been attended to, and you turn to the inner life—well, if you don't know where it is or what it is, you'll be sorry."

When a developer throws a company printer (otherwise known as an *asset*) to the floor because the print job has stalled yet again, and then picks it up and drops it again, it isn't because the communal bowl of mood elevators has not been refilled. When you have to call security to have your most productive programmer physically restrained from repeatedly slamming a technical support's face into the keyboard after his code was deleted days before the deadline, it isn't because he has anger issues. It is because modern software management theories have created one of the most bizarre, psychologically twisted workplace environments in modern times.

Given the physical appearance of the typical cube farm, the deprivation from natural world sights, sounds, and smells, and a culture that equates hours logged with value as a human, it shouldn't surprise at least a few readers that many developers feel like prisoners shackled with golden handcuffs. The only environments in which most developers ply their trade are nearly uniformly depressing, and the pressure to sacrifice all to the cause of the project is ubiquitous.

"Get out, then! Leave!" one might be tempted to say, but is it reasonable to expect of developers a withdrawal from a livelihood in which the skills are so specialized and refined that they would have great difficulty thriving in any other industry? Would you take a job just above minimum wage and start all over if you had even a glimmer of hope that things might someday change for the better?

An employee can be one of the WHOLE PEOPLE(8) in life only when her job and peers become a welcome part of her life, rather than some necessary evil with which she must contend to feed her family or some spell she has fallen under that promises options and an early retirement. Geeks are often singularly valued for the black magic they seem to invoke and their ability to crank code when called upon. How can you be the kind of leader who knows her team as multidimensional people with value that supersedes their craft?

Here are a few suggestions: Ask a team member to share her unique knowledge with the group in an informal setting, such as a lunch or a brown-bag talk or something totally spontaneous. Finding out who the gourmet cook is in your crowd or who parachutes out of airplanes every Saturday can tell you a lot about the people you work with. And getting them to talk about their pastime activities can make them feel whole and respected for more than just their incredible socket layer code. When you introduce them to new clients or new members of the company, throw in a personal detail or two. Yes, occasionally there will be someone who has a desire to keep his outside life to himself. Respect that, too, but at least ask once. Just ask once. That might be all it takes. And for you managers who just can't put down the dry, performance-oriented human management books, look up *relationship building*. Is it there?

You are perfectly positioned to help return humanity to the cold world of business, management, and code.

> Therefore:
> Take concrete steps to learn about and acknowledge the aspirations of your employees. In doing so, you will come to recognize their personal priorities, and they will know that you regard them as people rather than as just "heads" in your staffing profile. You will help to create personal networks of individuals and thereby stronger companies by treating your developers as whole people.

WHOLE PEOPLE(8) is closely related to patterns regarding the work environment, such as LIVING SPACE(53), PRIVATE SPACE(56), and PUBLIC SPACE(57). Even though we amuse ourselves with patterns such as GEEK CHANNELING(12)—and we fully embrace the contradictory nature of our order—we will all fail without TOTAL COMMITMENT(2).

Native American chiefs Frank Seelatse and Chief Jimmy Noah Saluskin of the Yakima tribe posed with the US Capitol behind them, 1927. Photographer unknown.

9

Cultural Competence

. . . creating diversity in the world, and in the organization as its microcosm, must mean more than tolerating cultural difference. It's about the nature of our relationships to the others in our environment.[1]

In the global, modern, high-tech workplace, equal opportunity and legislation have allowed many people the chance to contribute. Yet, even the operational enforcement of equal opportunity is based on assumptions about certain groups of people. Only true diversity will allow all of us to contribute to our fullest ability.

Library of Congress Prints & Photographs Division [LC-USZ62-92917 DLC and LC-USZ62-111354 DLC].

1. We gratefully acknowledge Jude Smith (hazelburymanor@hotmail.com), diversity trainer and author, for her contributions toward educating us about why diversity is so much more than a simple management issue.

Are you the kind of manager who, after years of "sensitivity training" led by your human resources department, knows exactly what the rules are when dealing with specifically enumerated groups of people, such as ethnic minority groups, disabled persons, or women? You are probably acutely aware of what the rules are and how to stay out of deep trouble. Depending on your point of view, you may think it's very nice that more people are being educated and finding equal opportunity, but you personally draw the line at someone telling you whom you're going to hire because your company has to get its "diversity numbers" up.

Solely focusing on equal opportunity issues may be where the effort first began to break down—regulation, legislation, affirmative action, special focus on minority recruiting, or any well-intentioned efforts are not really about creating diversity. Mandates to create diversity in the workplace are not ends within themselves. In some companies, diversity as nothing more than any practice of blame may have done more to promote feelings of threat and potential loss among all workers than to promote the true benefits that diversity will bring.

Work is more than just the place we spend nearly all of our waking hours as described in WHOLE PEOPLE(8)—it is a social interaction, a virtual petri dish of group behavior. Although people coming into software development organizations have probably already done a great deal of assimilation through their education and previous jobs, their individual identities, borne of their experiences, do not disappear completely. Recognizing that we each put on our own individual filters every morning is key. And yet, we believe that the simplest forms of awareness that can lead to CULTURAL COMPETENCE(9) are not difficult to have. It is as simple as this:

> *Never, ever, assume that you are the baseline measurement for the definition of what is different. You're not.*

In some Native American tribal cultures, a sign of humility and respect is to offer a limp hand in a handshake with another. If that other is someone acculturated to the high-powered corporate notion of a strong grip and hearty pump to a handshake as the measure of a person, both people are going to walk away completely misunderstanding what has happened. Rather than immediately assuming that one's opposite in this transaction is either weak and passive or overbearing and disrespectful, an openness to meaning other than the obvious one as prescribed by the dominant culture may be wonderfully instructive. And what about those interminable meetings that never seem to get anywhere: Men's style of interaction is characterized by interruption of one another with no offense taken, whereas women tend to listen politely and wait for natural openings in the conversation. Women may tend to shut down in such an environment, especially when there are no apparent natural openings. And if a woman does stomp on the conversation, well, we all know what people call her behind her back. Think of the information lost to this organization and the human relationships that comprise it. The bottom line is that lack of awareness can cost you dearly.

Think about these things:

◆ When you were born—Baby Boomer, Depression era, Gen X, or Gen Y

◆ Where you were born

◆ Your religious experience

◆ Your family experience—extended, two-parent household, or single parent

◆ The social and economic environment of your childhood

◆ The national and world events you experienced

◆ Ceremonies of your culture

◆ Who you thought was beautiful, handsome, or frightening

How were you shaped? What is your story? What were the circumstances of your forming into adulthood? If it is hard to really isolate these things, consider what social workers and anthropologists have known for a long time: Culture is largely hidden, not obvious. It manifests itself in ideas of beauty; in notions of subordination; in conversational patterns; in ideas of play and work; in concepts of justice; in approaches to leadership; in use or suspicion of consensus; in perception of time; and in many, many other areas that reflect our core values and self-understanding. Take the time to understand yourself and your complex personality—individuals are more than skin color, gender, and ethnicity. There are far more elements that make up each person, and it's quite possible that our commonalties overlap more frequently than our differences.

Therefore:
Understand what your own values are, and most especially your limitations and prejudices. When you react strongly to another person, understand why you might be having this reaction. Engage those who are different from you

and those who irritate you most profoundly with a sincere desire to learn and see from a different point of view, if only for the moment. Open the dialogue in your teams about your differences and end the unhelpful silence.

Display of shoes in front of store, Crowley, Louisiana.

10

Hover Shoes

. . . managing chaos can be frustrating. Just viewing a landscape polluted with infighting, politics, and emotional wreckage can be paralyzing. It is human instinct to deny confusion and upheaval, especially when it affects our zone of responsibility. It is also human instinct to relentlessly parse, understand, and control elements of our reality, even when they are completely outside our sphere of influence.

Many managers in technology, whether in large corporations or edgy start-ups, are faced with varying degrees of disorder and discord. From one week to the next, leadership changes, or even when leadership doesn't change the chain of decision making can be complete nonsense. Protecting yourself and your team members from the accompanying condition of corporate vertigo is difficult.

Photographed by Russell Lee, 1938; Library of Congress, Prints & Photographs Division, FSA-OWI Collection [LC-USF33-011700-M5 DLC].

A five-year-old boy we know was discussing inventions of the future and mentioned how useful a pair of HOVER SHOES would be. Especially if one's room was messy, you could put on your hover shoes, which would create pillows of air under your feet actuated by motors in the soles (okay, he didn't exactly describe it like that, but that's the general idea as translated by a habitual engineer), providing just enough "hover" to lift you above the piles of rubbish and thereby provide the ability to avoid squashing anything of value or injuring your own feet. Anyone who has ever stepped on one of those little metal cars knows exactly what we are talking about. Likewise, any manager who has stumbled over controversy knows that he needs a pair of those hover shoes.

Quick shifts in corporate policy and direction are deadening to engineering enthusiasm. Any developer who has worked diligently on a system only to discover at the end of the long haul that the customer they thought had never expressed more than polite interest over drinks to your business lead, will certainly not be carrying the torch of enthusiasm into your next project. Just when you feel you have engendered your developers' interest and sense of challenge for your newest gig, the client changes the whole thrust or throws in a bunch of bizarre features. You have done your due diligence with your customers (PUSH THE CUSTOMER(26)), but you cannot control the whole chain of events that might affect your work, your raise pool, or other artifacts of wayward company policy. You can spend all day trying to meet your client's needs, only to be faced back at the office by a bunch of dour developers who sniff at your effort. If you don't attempt to control the chaos, who will?

We all know managers who seem to swap from one crisis to another without ever really accomplishing anything. One manager in the aviation industry would get so breathless running from one issue to the next, that she was blue enough to require oxygen between sprints. Carmen Stefanopolis (not her real name) had been around for years, having clawed her way up the corporate ladder at Flyboy International from administrative assistant to a manager in technical support. Her customers weren't people having problems with their word-processing macros, these were engineers who were trying to create, build, and install life-protecting safety systems for real-time flight operations. Her staff was comprised of some of the most intelligent hackers around—they thought fast, they moved fast, and they took massive quantities of blame whenever a backup tape failed or a machine's inodes became hopelessly scrambled.

In her office, she sat among three-foot-high stacks of paper, her computer bleeped with incoming mail, and the screen flickered with each incoming message.

Every request that she received was carefully filtered by her and doled out to whoever she felt was most appropriate. After assigning this responsibility, she watched her staff, waiting to see what the resolution would be. *Every* problem, from the printer paper being out to the demo machines crashing, carried equal opportunity for hysteria. Needless to say, her hotshot team of computer jocks and system programmers hated her guts. Doors slammed all up and down the hall for emergency complaining sessions, and one programmer visibly shook with the effort of self-control whenever Carmen walked into the room. The situation got so bad that the corporate leadership actually noticed, and finally a management consultant was called in.

We have a friend who insists that cleaning the bathroom is very satisfying. It smells good after you finish cleaning, the mirrors look like you can reach through them, the faucets shine, and the porcelain gleams. Unlike any other cleaning activity in the house, you can really see the net effect of your scrubbing and buffing. We realized how sane her comments actually are. She was choosing to take on the effort that she actually had a chance of success with. Cleaning the kitchen was only momentarily satisfying—until the next kid came through and tossed his crumbs on the counter. Vacuuming leaves behind invisible microbes, and making the bed lasts only until the next nap. For the moments when life was most stressful, when the house was a wreck, and when people were making chronically unreasonable demands on her sanity, she could be found scrubbing the toilet bowl.

Just what do toilet bowls, Carmen Stefanopolis, and air-powered shoes have to do with managing chaos? You don't have to try to clean up all the messes, all of the time. A problem directly relevant to the success of your current project deserves your attention; distracting speculation and concern about factors outside of your direct control can be ignored indefinitely. Systematically and purposefully ignore the insignificance and petty politics around you, and focus on the problems that require your attention.

> Therefore:
> Stay a few feet above the wreckage by taking time to evaluate which problems require your attention now, which can wait until later, and which are completely absurd.

◆◆◆

This pattern is closely associated with SWITZERLAND(6) and INOCULATION(28) in helping you to decide which concerns deserve priority.

The Wukoki Ruin at Wupatki National Monument, Arizona. The blowhole is actually at the Wupatki ruin, but it's not much to look at, really—it's just a hole in the ground.

11

Blowhole

. . . nature loves a state of equilibrium. In northern Arizona, at the Wupatki National Monument preservation site, a deep crack in the earth has become exposed to the air through a small cleft in the surface crust. On a hot day, one can stand above the hole and feel cool air rushing out as the denser molecules surge to fill the space left by the disparate molecules that comprise the warmer ambient air. Conversely, on a cold day, the air is sucked downward, into the warmer cavity for the same reason. And on a day that is neither really cool nor hot, nothing perceptible happens at all. It is called the blowhole.

Managing clients and a team of software developers can make one feel an awful lot like a human blowhole. Constantly trying to fill the empty spaces as your corporate leadership, clients, and team blow hot and cold can make one feel absolutely breathless. Yet, not maintaining equilibrium between your customers and developers will allow an imbalance that releases with such a force that you will be either sucked into the chasm of failure or blown into the ozone of irrelevance.

Many leaders we have worked with seem to struggle with this notion of allegiance. Who owns you? The people with the big money that ultimately butter your bread and can pull you up that big ladder of power, or that team of hotshot developers that nag you, complain frequently, but hold your very success in their hands? How do you deal with being in a constant state of tension, pulled between the feeling of obligation you have toward those who first offered you your title of Director, Manager, or Distinguished Member of Technical Staff, and the day-to-day struggle to lead your team who depends on you.

It is a lack of corporate equilibrium that pits the software developer against all other interests—especially the sales and marketing department. It is because of the extreme loss of balance between these very differently motivated forces. Unfortunately, you're the portal between these competing interests. Companies will market and sell themselves as the purveyors of a specific technology that has never been built or designed—yet, somehow, at the end of the day, it's always the engineers who take it in the shorts when the product isn't delivered on time.

That a project was a complete failure doesn't even seem to stop the really driven sales and marketing blowhards. We know an engineer who was called in to write a case study of a trial for a new routing technology used by a large access provider. The trial was a total flop—the machines crashed, the software was the wrong revision, and the entire support staff where the trial was being conducted loathed the high-maintenance needs of the product. When the engineer complained that it was impossible to write a positive case study of a failed installation, the marketing staff patiently explained that this was a critical contract and the study had to be done. Perhaps he could just take some of his less than complimentary quotes and use "some of those ellipsis things" to take out the negative stuff so it sounded better. And then, as if the marketing lead had just awakened from a narcoleptic attack, she chimed in, "Just explain how they were really hurting and how we helped them with their points of pain."

Of course, the marketing staff thought the engineer was just trying to stir up trouble, as engineers are often known to do, and requested someone else on the job. The engineer felt like the last defender of truth and justice in a world of lies and spam, and wanted the project and the client to be entirely denied. Meanwhile, with both ears being tugged mercilessly, his manager was being pushed by marketing to bring in more money to the company and to figure out how to make this very wealthy client happy.

Famous British novelist and poet Thomas Hardy wrote:

THE SUBALTERNS

I

"Poor wanderer," said the leaden sky,
"I fain would light thee,
But there are laws in force on high
Which say it must not be."

II

—"I would not freeze thee, shorn one," cried
The North, "Knew I but how
To warm my breath, to slack my stride;
But I am ruled as thou."

III

—"To-morrow I attack thee, wight,"
Said sickness. "Yet I swear
I bear thy little ark no spite,
But I am bid enter there."

IV

—"Come hither, Son." I heard death say;
"I did not will a grave
Should end thy pilgrimage to-day,
But I, too, am a slave!"

V

We smiled upon each other then,
And life to me had no less
Of that fell look it wore ere when
They owned their passiveness.

Like Thomas Hardy's narrator, you may have powerful, though innocent, forces raging all around you. You will have to smile on each and balance them out, absorbing in yourself the forces that surround you. As a leader, you must equalize the forces if you ever want to experience calm in your future days.

Therefore:

When you understand the facets of the problem, make a decision, and follow through to establish equilibrium among the competing interests. Equalize the pressure. This may require giving a little here, a little there, absorbing a little yourself, and finding the point where the pressures balance. Being a BLOW-HOLE is what can prevent the need for DIRECT ACTION(19), where you might have to get intrusive on the one hand, or jumping to FALL ON THE GRENADE(51), where you might have to suck up all the injury yourself.

Being an effective human BLOWHOLE(11), means understanding how to PUSH THE CUSTOMER(26), and position yourself as SWITZERLAND(6) with a pair of HOVER SHOES(10) strapped on.

Forked stick twists and points downward in water witch's hands over proper location for well. Pie Town, New Mexico.

12

Geek Channeling

. . . the correct focus can sometimes reveal things hidden to the naked eye.

You are responsible for keeping your team in the corporate loop and from spinning into random directions. Everybody's busy.

You schedule important organizational meetings, but your developers rarely show up, claiming they have *work to do*. But their *work* seems to be more concerned with discovering the newest killer application, eradicating heisenbugs (see TRIBAL LANGUAGE(17)) in their software, or dissing the latest Internet worm that took down all of Europe's computers as "juvenile." You've tried it all—they don't respond to threats, e-mail hassles, or high-priority meeting requests. And although they seem hopelessly out of touch with reality, they have enough of their wits about them to

Photograph by Russell Lee, 1940; Library of Congress, Prints & Photographs Division, FSA-OWI Collection [LC-USF33-012751-M3 DLC].

manage puts and calls on high-tech stocks in real-time from their Personal Digital Assistants.

Perhaps it is true that your software developers really do not care about the company's survival, unless they have options that haven't vested yet. We all know that high-tech jobs are not in short supply, and that there is always a new company angling to raid your best employees. You sense that your grumpy developers are really just trying to find a way to enjoy themselves in the passage of a day—not only are your developers nothing more than sole proprietors with you as their primary client, but any really bad news is greeted with giddy delight at the coming chaos that will descend on the organization. Ever wonder why? Your developers are in it for their enjoyment of the game, and your meetings and corporate messages are distracting from the fun.

But what seems to be a total breakdown in discipline and submission to power is actually something rare and wonderful. You have somehow managed to find yourself in an enviable position. Really. You need only learn how to communicate effectively with your independent, freewheeling thinkers. You are lucky that you have a team that has the spine and creative chutzpah to turn your corporate model on its head.

Stimulating bored or apathetic people is much, much harder than channeling those already filled with passion.

If you let these people run roughshod over you, you could have the most powerful, ingenious, creative team your company has ever seen.

Chinese philosopher Hung Tzu Ch'eng (1593–1665) made the comment, "Human affairs are like a chess game; only those who do not take it seriously can be called good players." One author had a manager that understood these words precisely. On several occasions, the corporate busybodies ordered employees to watch a video or study a document on compliance, corporate manners, or filling out time sheets correctly (see OUTCOME BASED(20)). Accompanying the order would be a sheet on which each member of the team would sign his or her name, indicating that he or she had an opportunity to view, read, or otherwise ingest the required propaganda. The manager read it quite literally, as he stood in front of the team, held the video up, and stated, "I'm required to give you the opportunity to view this video on the corporate beer-at-lunch policy. Does anyone want this?" He looked around at each of the faces in the room, "No, then, please sign this sheet indicating you were offered the opportunity." Then he promptly tossed the video in the trash.

By the way, this team managed to garner almost all of the highly prized strategic money doled out every year and turned out some of the hottest software and the best beer by far on our company-funded, secret, team-building brewing missions.

Larry Constantine, renegade author of *Constantine on Peopleware,* calls this "breaking through":[1]

> Instead of putting stability ahead of change, instability is promoted, becoming the driving force to overcome blindly accepted practices and unquestioned notions. Instead of putting corporate and collective interests above individual ones, individual freedom of expression and action come first. Where the traditional pyramid tries to rein in cantankerous coding "cowboys" and "cowgirls," breakthrough teams love them and let them run free. This freewheeling atmosphere stimulates creativity and tends to promote the "personal best" performances that generate breakthroughs.

Try a little breakthrough action of your own: Come on, close the door, kneel down on your special pillow, palms upward, eyes rolled to the back of your skull, and receive the geeks. Let their voices travel through you. Feel the beam of focus penetrate you with the message to *deny* unwanted proclamations or bureaucratic necessities.

Abuse instant messaging and blast your team with a misguided joke, encode your message in MP3, or add a hot link to the team web page[2] (which will make them think you're possibly human after all). It should be obvious by now—don't bother with e-mail or calendar software, as your team has already filtered out any messages with the word IMPORTANT in the subject line. Haven't you noticed that the only reply you ever get on your calendar software is on the days when their archiving robot dumps them all into the bit bucket?

Therefore:
Think Geek! Your developers are lifting your 193-pound nut-and-bolt, and the only way you are going to reach them now is with a 193-pound nut-and-bolt

---

1. Constantine, Larry (1995). *Constantine on Peopleware.* Englewood Cliffs, NJ: Yourdon Press, 66.
2. Please check your company's policies before doing something like this. You don't want to lose your job by adding an inappropriate link. If the link you insert simply leads to a "Gotcha!" page that says something like, "Caught you, you dirty little skankenheimer!", the geeks will at least appreciate your humor.

wrench swinging from your belt. Devise ways to communicate with your engineers that are on their terms and within their comfort zone.

◆◆◆

GEEK CHANNELING(12) is best supported by a clear understanding of the use of TRIBAL LANGUAGE(17) and LEVIATHAN(3) within the subculture of your geek team. You can't fake effective GEEK CHANNELING(12), nor should it be attempted by the faint of heart.

Using a 2000-pound steam hammer on jar rein for drilling equipment. Keystone Drilling Company, Beaver Falls, Pennsylvania.

Photographed by John Vachon ,1941; Library of Congress, Prints & Photographs Division, FSA-OWI Collection [LC-USF34-062243-D DLC].

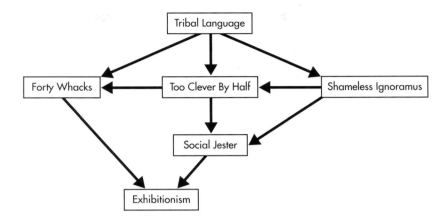

II

Behavioral and Expulsive Patterns

The Psychological and Retentive Patterns described in Part I represent ways of thinking that can be internalized, whereas the patterns in this part manifest themselves in outward behavior. Based upon the belief that to be an effective leader one must first squarely recognize the reality of the situation, these patterns expose the forces behind those who live software development and show how the courageous can use this gained knowledge to their benefit. If there is any common thread running through them, it is this: Be bold in your manner. Whether a fool, a sage, or a warrior, management is not a place to be reclusive. You must reveal your-self, and if a tendency toward the hermetic is how you are wired, then it might be wise to strive to overcome that propensity, at least in small ways and gestures, to let your true capabilities shine through.

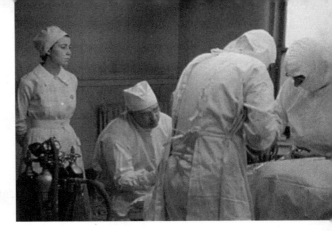

Operation, Herrin Hospital (private), Herrin, Illinois.

13

Exhibitionism

. . . prior to the twentieth century, surgeons often practiced with great exhibitionist flair, laying open the innards of their patients for all to witness— the act of surgery was a resplendent and extravagant display of surgical prowess. The individualist in his medical theater was master of his dominion. Unfortunately for the patient on the table, these kinds of individualist theatrics often led to grave infection or simply caused the patient to bleed to death.

You are sincere in your TOTAL COMMITMENT(2) to your team. Conveying this commitment to them, however, is a puzzling and difficult endeavor.

Photograph by Arthur Rothstein, 1939; Library of Congress, Prints & Photographs Division, FSA-OWI Collection [LC-USF33-002971-M1 DLC].

You want to lead your team to success, but instead you feel as if you are selling your soul to the corporation, your very life, and gaining only self-disgust, anxiety, and perhaps living with depression. (Think we're being dramatic here? Take a mood-elevating drug poll in your company and mail us the results.) In fact, you want to do more than succeed; you want your day-to-day existence to mean something. Frankly, things just aren't going that great for you as a manager with a bunch of high-tech mavericks on your team. In fact, you realize that you are pretty ineffective in general. You are making some headway with some of your projects; others wither on the vine; most just spin helplessly out of control. No one seems to like you, laugh at your jokes, or revere you in the slightest. You've tried management effectiveness courses, togetherness sessions, and overpaid feel-good consultants whose mere presence seemed to exacerbate the entire situation.

It is time to demonstrate your best chops as a manager, to flourish your cape before the charging bull, to wield your scalpel skillfully into your own viscera! A little EXHIBITIONISM could be the salve you need.

We're not really talking about a big sob session with your team or a dramatic Zorroesque battle with your foes. Rather, we are talking about a shift from *acting* like a manager to leading with genuine attitude of sincerity and flair. (Besides, a crying or romantically masked manager can be pretty unnerving for a tribe of often socially repressed software developers.) We're talking about honest dialogue and an end to management paradigms worldwide. It's hard. Most of us fail initially when we try to break the mold, but as a leader you can set the pace. It takes guts. Nothing is in shorter supply than inspiration.

A fumbling department at an oversized disk-drive manufacturer was assembled to have a heartfelt dialogue about the company president's vision. Not surprisingly, this turned out to be the typical claptrap such as, "Exceeding customer expectations while bringing dignity and prosperity to our employees and maximizing profits for our shareholders."

The manager tasked with the hopeless role of leading this travesty, whom we'll call Alice, tried with great but false earnestness to engender the discussion, because she felt it was her job. In fact, the way the director had framed it for her, she had been offered up this session as a great opportunity to prove her "leadership" qualities. The fact was that he couldn't foist it off on anyone else, and as the only woman in a managing position in his department, he liked turning the heat up on her to see if she could handle it. Alice, who was by nature a cheerful and upbeat person, and yet a true believer in her corporate mission, started the meeting by reading the president's vision statement, which we'll summarize here (and spare our dear readers) as platitudinous excrement. She looked back from the slide projected on the screen to the developers arrayed across the small auditorium. For those who knew Alice well, it was already a heartbreaking moment.

"So, everyone, what do you think of the president's vision?"

As if of one mind, there was a collective sigh, a closing of eyes, and a gentle shaking of all the heads in the room. One of the developers, in his first ever opportunity to quote Shakespeare in a corporate environment, said, from *Hamlet,* "Words, words, words." (Okay, for the two literary purists reading this book, it is a little out of context, although Hamlet did indeed utter them to Polonius, who was one windy son of a gun.)

Despite the apparent hopelessness of her position, opportunity was knocking for Alice, and on a scale that could have vaulted her to the highest halls in the pantheon of beloved managers. Although many developers liked Alice personally, they were wary of her cheerleading for the company, viewing it as terribly insincere, shamelessly ambitious, or frightfully delusional. Here, on a silver platter, was a chance to show what she was really made of, and for whom she really labored. A ripe fruit hung there for a moment, aglow in its perfection.

All she had to do was let her hair down and admit, yes, it was a lot of sententious garbage and couldn't we just give it the stamp of approval and move on? But she didn't. She tried, vainly, to justify this vacant and useless exercise that required the presence of dozens of engineers, most of whom chafed to get back to their real work. Her scuffling and repeated equivocations made her lack of sincerity overwhelmingly evident. The real tragedy was that deep down, this was not at all what Alice was made of, but she failed in that moment to provide the spark that would blow this stinking hypocrisy to kingdom come. To all those developers, she became the stooge that they feared she might be.

Consequently, her credibility and integrity suffered horribly that day and never really recovered. Her honesty was compromised because she was now viewed as a lackey and corporate climber at worst, and a gutless dishrag at best. To make it worse, she whined about her ungrateful developers to her boss, who later scolded the same department for not taking the "vision exercise" more seriously. Her being a stooge, first validated, was now etched in the stony memories of the crowd. Who would ever want to follow her now? When she moved up or sideways or out of the company altogether, who would clamor to be taken along, assured of her honesty, nerve, and guardianship of truth?

Naturally, the karmic wheel of middle managers turned again as the next reorganization came and crushed many poor saps on its route. Alice was shifted hither and yon, and finally left the company altogether—a company to which she had given all her working years since college. Oh, and the vision statement? It was rewritten two or three more times before being abandoned altogether. Apparently the president's vision was uncorrectable, the result, no doubt, of a vision disorder.

Like the exhibitionist surgeons of the nineteenth century, you are opening up your team to some potentially pernicious problems for them and you. You are no longer choosing to play the corporate game, and that can be very dangerous, especially in the short term. In the long term, however, you'll find that you will have rediscovered your integrity, and that will carry you further than your next bonus check. The relationships that survive your move to radical sincerity will be relationships solidly founded, and your successes will be the result of your leadership, not your machinations.

Therefore:
When forced or duped into leading pointless exercises that are really just a box some executive wants to check in a long list of objectives, check your pulse. That's right—put your hand against your chest, feel for your heart, see if it's still beating. If you find yourself running around the office looking for a defibrillator, then we've got the electric shock for you. It's time to come clean; it's time to tell the truth and to become an exhibitionist of sincerity. If you suspect it's nonsense, then it's time to call it nonsense. It's a near guarantee that your developers will certainly smell it. We're pretty short of offering religion or words to live by, but we can tell you that if you can dig down and serve up some real stuff, your resolve and strength to become an effective leader will harden.

Being seen as a human being rather than a corporate lackey is a very important step toward earning respect from people. If it takes you down a peg or two in the pantheon of the corporate hierarchy, you won't miss it; at least, since you've gotten this far in the book, we suspect you're above your fear of losing your latest foothold. The roots of neurosis are in saying one thing while believing another. Knock it off. Align your words with your beliefs.

President Franklin D. Roosevelt; photo by Office of War Information, 1941.

14

Shameless Ignoramus

"We have nothing to fear, but fear itself."—Franklin Delano Roosevelt

. . . the complexity of today's software development climate feels like a tidal wave about to overcome you. As a manager, it seems impossible to fight the undertow of obsolescence; yet it is essential that you become comfortable with walking the thin line between the contempt and respect that emanate from your developers.

Developers seem to speak in a vernacular that is completely foreign to you, and, as to the deeper technical details of things, you are lost. Even though you were once a whizbang engineer yourself, back in the days of 8-bit CPUs, the speed of change has left you with an almost total lack of comprehension of the technology. You must understand the scope of the project to fulfill its goals successfully.

The minute you open up your mouth to discuss the latest mutation in requirements with your team, you are gripped by the fear of sounding utterly idiotic. With a team of individuals who seem to know so much more than you, who maintain concrete skills, and who understand project complexities, it seems only a matter of time before you are left behind and rendered useless.

It is a truly terrifying thing to let slip one's grip on the tools of production that put the bread and butter on the table, that bought new pairs of shoes for baby, and that, hopefully, will send that baby to college. Some managers valiantly attempt to stay on the edge of everything new, sucking up journals and surfing developer web sites such as slashdot to at worst master the jargon and at best to be able to roll up their sleeves and hack some code. In fact, this quest for quick-and-dirty comprehension is what the manager hopes will ultimately win the respect of her developers.

There is just one problem. Management, of and by itself, is a full-time job. It is as if some weird offshoot of Parkinson's Law of Data has overtaken your existence:

Data will always expand to fill the space

becomes for you:

Inane requests will always expand to fill every spare moment of your day.

The free moment you'd like to use for technical study suddenly fills up with meetings; seminars; conference calls; crisis abatement; peer reviews; action plans; unplanned presentations; consultant interviews; budget tussles; breakfast meetings with the CEO; lunches with an executive VP; customer entertaining; plans and replans; scheduling wrangles; new software upgrades; a switchover to a new e-mail system; brawls with the color printer; and all the drop-in traffic that needs this or that signed, noted, inspected, or deferred. In between, your telephone rings, punctuated by your pager, and even when you exit the restroom stall after a 15-minute "meditation," you are accosted by someone with a problem before you even reach the sink to wash your hands. None of this is conducive to the study of new technology, unless you want totally to give up any semblance of a normal life. But even if you could somehow find the time to learn all the technical skills and know-how to apply them, how wise would that be? If no single technical person can grasp the nature of the LEVIATHAN(3), then how are you going to do it?

Common sense tells us that no leader can have all the answers. In most work groups, problems are too numerous and too complex to be solved by the resources of the leader alone. This is as true for technical (job-related) problems as it is for human problems, which are often more complex—particularly when it concerns a personal problem of a group member or an interpersonal conflict between two members.[1]

Wait a minute. Dr. Thomas Gordon, quoted here in his 1977 work, *Leadership Effectiveness Training,* says that technical problems may not even be the most difficult, and here you may be, boning up on material that won't even help you address the toughest problems you'll encounter. Is there no end to these burdens?

Some of us may remember the great American peanut farmer and president, Jimmy Carter. President Carter was amazing in his ability to master arcane details of nearly every facet of government work. So profound was his intelligence and grasp of the minutiae of the executive branch's departments that he was satirized on the popular weekly American comedy show *Saturday Night Live* as understanding even the workings of an obscure postal machine's innards. Unfortunately for President Carter, and perhaps for the country, he lost himself in this detail and failed to understand some of the larger issues at play during his administration.

Carter had the common leader's belief that if you shepherded all the technical details correctly, the big picture would find focus itself, and all would be well. Unfortunately, he was soundly defeated in the next election by a Hollywood actor renowned for admitting, and even celebrating, his complete ignorance of the pesky little details. We're not suggesting you adopt the ultrahigh-level visions of Ronald Reagan and ignore *every* last detail, but rather that you strike a balance. When it comes to deeper technical matters, leave them wholly to your developers. Trust them implicitly as your experts in their areas or they may leave you to your own devices, which can really spell disaster.

Therefore:
Give up the attempt to know it all. Become a SHAMELESS IGNORAMUS(14) when it comes to detailed technical matters. Even when you happen to grasp what is going on technically, you stand to learn even more by not overpowering your developers simply by virtue of your position rather than by your comprehension. Ask questions when you need clarification and shamelessly leave behind the details when they are not required for you to function successfully.

1. Gordon, Thomas (1977). *Leadership Effectiveness Training.* New York, G. P. Putnam's Sons, 46.

Your developers, contrary to the traditional geek contempt for those not technically savvy, will appreciate your candor, or at least your ability to listen. They will remember to clue you in to what is really important. If they appreciate you, they will defend your penchant to look foolish. Because of their desire to be appreciated, the more articulate developers will try to frame their explanations to you in plain terms that you can translate to the corporate giants. Best of all, you may avoid the pitfalls of being TOO CLEVER BY HALF(15).

This is going to take a little faith and the ability to GET A GURU(21). Truly yielding to the LEVIATHAN(3) and understanding TRIBAL LANGUAGE(17) may actually be a great relief for you. You can become the SOCIAL JESTER(18) to frame a declaration of technical vacancy, as opposed to just looking lost and drooling a little bit.

*Houdini and the water torture
cell, 1913.*

15

Too Clever by Half

. . . *everyone wants to be seen as smart, and some people are indeed smarter
than others. Cleverness and wit are valuable tools, but like knives, fire, and
guns, they need to be wielded skillfully so no one feels intimidated and no
one gets hurt. We all admire brainy people, but we also should take into
account the Law of Unintended Consequences when considering how clever
we can be. The British, with a wise suspicion of overly smart people and
actions, have the expression "too clever by half" to describe those very smart
moves that result in some very unwanted outcomes. By the way, Harry Houdini died from complications arising from acute appendicitis after inviting a
fan to hit him in his iron-hard stomach.*

*The American Variety Stage: Vaudeville and Popular Entertainment, 1870–1920, Library of
Congress McManus-Young Collection [LC-USZ62-112434 DLC].*

◆◆◆

One burden of leadership is the feeling that you must always be a step ahead of everyone you manage and that you must create the impression of being the smartest of the bunch, whether or not this is actually the case.

Being a manager has its benefits, but it also places burdens on you, not the least of which is for you always to be informed, knowledgeable, quick-witted, and intellectually incisive. After all, if you're to lead, you have to be the best of the bunch, right?

As developers, we don't necessarily view our leaders as being our superiors in terms of technical knowledge, and certainly not in general intellectual acuity. Part of the reason for this is the natural cockiness that being an alpha geek requires, but it also comes from the recognition that our managers are where they are because they possess *different* skills than we possess and that—hopefully—those skills will benefit the parts of the project that are essential but that we have no interest in doing ourselves. We recognize, in good leaders at least, skills that are difficult to develop, which do not have specific and testable outcomes, unlike most of the production in hightech. Some of us even realize the many and varied pressures that our managers are under from disparate quarters and how absolutely mind numbing some of the duties must be. We don't even like having to do our own personal development plans; having to help 37, or even 7, employees do theirs must be torture. Good managers do not have to prove that their jobs are more important than ours or that they are smarter than we are in doing our jobs.

Not that the more foolish haven't tried. We have had bosses who had a peculiar need to diminish the difficulty of the developer's role in order to elevate the importance of the management position. We've seen our leaders bobbing their heads every time we open our mouths as if what we are saying is hopelessly redundant. Other approaches include fobbing off the manager's own duties to developers, as if to illustrate by experience how tough it is to come up with a budget spreadsheet—"Okay, you do it." Well, it could be really tough, particularly if we don't know how to use a spreadsheet application in the first place, don't really care about your budget in the second place, and already have more than enough on our plates just to deliver the first release of software to system test.

This "fobbing off" was one of the unfortunate side effects of the *whole-team* approach to project management. In addition to doing all the technical development, engineers were saddled with scheduling, budget, staffing, risk management, quality assurance, and other duties that were once done by their managers. This didn't eliminate a level of management, of course, but it did create a whole new level of "unmanagers" who, being technically incompetent or disinterested, jumped at the opportunity to pester others and to avoid doing testable technical work at the same time. We still weren't self-directed in the end, but only made more liable for blame when things went wrong. These unmanagers, by the way, are identifiable by their unflagging ability to raise "issues" that never seem to fall to them to resolve, but fall, instead, to developers already sagging under the weight of their own responsibilities. But we digress. Keep in mind that with each act there is a corollary act—in this case, the Law of Unintended Consequences.

Our mental archives are jammed with memories of initiatives taken by well-meaning managers attempting to stay ahead of the curve. Here's a good one: At an aerospace company there was a management initiative to do all coding in Program Definition Language (PDL) first, before proceeding to actual code. A good idea, certainly, on its face. No one could argue with the intent, which was to catch design errors earlier in the development cycle as well as to have an implementation-neutral form in which to express the detailed design. The manager behind this initiative devoured the technical literature of the day extolling such breakthrough methodologies and felt himself far ahead of his reluctant programming staff in trying to reduce programming errors. But what was TOO CLEVER BY HALF was the strict requirement to keep all documentation and support materials synchronized with the living code. As the code evolved over many releases, it soon became apparent that however long it took to change the actual executable code, it took five times as long to change the PDL. This occurred for two reasons. First, the PDL ended up being more complex than the running code because it lacked many of the more powerful constructs of an actual computer programming language. Second, the purveyor of the tools used to create and maintain the PDL stopped supporting the particular platform then in use. Although the PDL could be written as simple text using any text editor, the tool they had been using had special capabilities and hidden notations, and stored the files in its own special database. When this platform's operating system went through the next major revision, the old PDL tools ceased to work at all, requiring special sessions in which the old operating system version was loaded to accommodate the use of the PDL tool. TOO CLEVER BY HALF!

When a manager tries to be more knowledgeable in the technical arena than the developers, it can blow up in any number of ways. The manager may end up overloaded in some cases. In other cases, the developers may feel that their little sliver of autonomy is being questioned, as they are peppered with questions and calls for justification in their approaches to doing the work. It's possible that a manager may mistakenly believe that he is a real expert when he is not, and end up in opposition to the team, trying to drive them this way or that. This is a particularly dangerous behavior to fall into because it costs you the respect of the team and earns, in its place, a seething resentment. Even if you *are* the expert, it doesn't pay in the long run to lord this over your staff. If you intimidate them, they will fear being creative, and even if they are not intimidated, they will weary of having you kibitz on work for which they hold the ultimate responsibility. Being the smartest one is fraught with perils. Beware the unintended consequences. Chant the words of Lau Tzu, "The wicked leader is he who the people despise. The good leader is he who the people revere. The great leader is he who the people say, 'We did it ourselves.'"

> Therefore:
> Apply your cleverness and wit to those areas in which the developers don't contribute and in which your mental dexterity will benefit them, not question or diminish them. Use your intellectual horsepower to get them what they need and to shield them from what they don't need. Downplay your expertise even when it really does exist, unless called upon by the team for specific help.

Check out the patterns SHAMELESS IGNORAMUS(14) and TOTAL COMMITMENT(2) as a way to balance this pattern.

Lizzie Borden, perhaps considering the miracle of indoor plumbing.

16

Forty Whacks

Lizzie Borden took an axe
And gave her Mother forty whacks
When she saw what she had done
She gave her father forty-one.

—Playground rhyme

. . . there is no direct evidence that Lizzie Borden murdered her parents, nor do any strong motives seem to exist. Still, many people theorize that Lizzie's bitter relationship with her father and stepmother may be at the heart of an explanation. Andrew Borden was condescendingly paternalistic, a notorious cheapskate who forced his family to live without indoor plumbing despite his wealth, and who allegedly took an unnatural interest in his daughter. Guilty or not (and a jury said "not"), it is clear that this family had a few unresolved issues. Consider this pattern carefully if you think of your development team as your family and of yourself as head of the household.

Fall River Police Department, 685 Pleasant Street, Fall River, MA 02721, http://www.frpd.org.

◆◆◆

You may find yourself unwilling to trust your developers or to turn your back on them even for a moment. You fear them talking about you to people outside the team. It's especially difficult for you to understand this dynamic when you feel that you honestly try to do what's best for them. Why are they such ungrateful children?

It's possible that you tend to think of your team as a family, although you might prefer a golden-age TV-family image to the image of the Borden's. After all, you spend so much time with the developers that you can't help expressing your parental instincts, desperately hoping to fulfill their needs with desires for their future happiness. You only ask that they behave when the time is critical and take care of you when you are feeble. And, sometimes, they act in accordance with those wishes, and sometimes, well, they embarrass you. You hope against hope that you don't have a Lizzie Borden lurking in your ranks, but sometimes you wonder.

Like many children, your software developers all seem to have their special demands, but never seem to remember the nice things that you do for them. They spend your money injudiciously, leave messes behind, and disappear just when you need them most. They vanish at critical times and forget to tell you where they're going; they decide they need a flex-day the day before your software release; they demand unsupported operating systems; and they request arcane training seminars. To make it all worse, they become irate or bitterly silent when you calmly explain to them why what they want is really not what they need.

Have you been nodding your head over the last few paragraphs? Is this your life? It's time to do something drastic and perhaps shocking, but for the good of your team and your project, it must be done. Ward Cleaver, from the seminal *Leave It to Beaver* series, is no longer your role model. We've fired him. The Cleaver family[1] is now going to operate as a collaborating group of adults. Heck, the Beaver is over 50 now, isn't he? Ward and June are rocking away cheerfully in the assisted-living center. And Eddie Haskell? He's the vice president of marketing and sales. Your developers don't need a parent, don't want a parent, and are going to operate much more

---

1. *Leave It to Beaver* was an American television show in the 1950s and 1960s. It featured perfect parents, Ward and June Cleaver; elder son Wally; and precocious but well meaning Theodore, who was called "The Beaver." Eddie Haskell was Wally's wise-guy friend.

creatively and productively and be happier when you remove that benevolent smile and condescending demeanor and treat them as competent *peers,* which is exactly what they are.

Depending on how far you have traveled down the paternalistic highway, you may have completely forgotten that you are dealing with fully functioning, productive, adult members of society. By refusing to treat them as adults, you have lost their respect, and they may quickly be losing their own self-respect. That's an ugly combination, and you may find them fighting back with the raised axe of noncompliance, by foot-dragging and backstabbing. Yes, somehow, things will just stop getting done.

You may be promulgating the attitude of your company, especially companies that walk in perpetual fear of employee lawsuits. Think about it: Does your company enforce the viewing of videos where two bad actors play good cop/bad cop over whether a beer with lunch is within "compliance." Does your company generate lots of paperwork and interactive web site activities that teach employees about your company's "standards of behavior," which involve not taking baseball tickets from customers? Chances are you have just become a mouthpiece for the corporate compliance department. Sure, there may not be any feasible way around the daylong sensitivity seminar, but you don't have to continue to convey the message that we are unable to behave in public. Even though the corporate mandate is that all employees must take the time-management class; if you find it ridiculous, don't pretend it's enlightening.

Steve McConnell, in describing why he believes teams fail, shares this anecdote:

> One young woman I know worked practically nonstop for 3 months to meet a deadline. When her product shipped, the manager thanked her in a fatherly way and gave her a stuffed animal. She thought the gesture was patronizing, and she was livid. . . .[2]

There are so many similar examples that we've heard from our fellow team members that we were shocked. Little pieces of paper that are premanufactured awards dumped out of Power Point are definitely on the 40-whack list, as are faux-granite sculptures and wooden ducks. Have you ever actually considered a heartfelt thank you (with a check if you have the budget) and genuine recognition? Even lunch with the team accompanied with gag gifts that somehow convey your understanding of the team member's individual experience, struggles, and contribution is

---

2. McConnell, Steve (1996). *Rapid Development.* Redmond, WA: Microsoft Press, 290.

more satisfying than a whole ream of Power Point awards. One manager we know thanked her team with a fabulous four-star dinner and gifts—such as a bottle of cheap wine for one particularly stressed out individual and a Mr. Potato Head for another who had been dealing with a morphing customer.

By comprehending that your parental treatment is the antecedent to your team's behavior, it should be obvious that you need to alter your point of view. By treating your software developers as children, they are responding exactly in the expected fashion. This is not a family, and while the uglier dynamics of our childhood do seem to rear up occasionally (as, dear reader, do yours), your paternalism is noticed and just downright offensive. Parental governance strips away the trust that is gained by your developers' expression of personal rights and responsibilities. Begin by finding opportunities that return those rights and responsibilities.

> Therefore:
> If you can somehow cut the paternalistic act and relate to your engineers as peers—yes, as adults—then they will be much more inclined to treat you with the respect that your performance, not your position, deserves. And don't adults make better engineers than children? At least they can drive themselves home.

This pattern works hand-in-hand with WHOLE PEOPLE(8), DRAMA(4), and METAPHOR(5), in which you round out who you all are, what you all are doing and why, and what the overriding shape of your working relationship is.

Chief Red Cloud, 1909.

17

Tribal Language

. . . Red Cloud was one of the greatest of the Lakota leaders of the nineteenth century. He was known for his ability to tell stories in an exciting and convincing manner, which is considered by some to be as much the key to his success as his strength in battle.

Developers contrive and use vernacular that can be cryptic and even evasive at times, yet if you are to really feel the pulse of the project, you must have some insight into what is actually being parleyed.

You are responsible for overseeing and managing one or more software-centered products. You have in your group or department a collection of competent engineers who are reliable and who deliver solid software products. Yet you are constantly annoyed because they seem to speak in a vernacular of their own that is

National Library of Congress Reproduction Number X-31871, Library of Congress.

completely comprehensible to them, but which is unintelligible chatter to you. You can never tell whether you are getting a straight answer, whether you are being dodged, or whether you are being completely insulted. How can you lead if you don't know what the story is? How can you track the project status if you can't even get a basic Yes or No answer to even the simplest of questions? The following dialogue will sound familiar to you:

YOU, THE MANAGER: "Hey, when is the test software going to be ready?"

YOUR DEVELOPER: "Well, I'm having trouble with the communications routine. I'm seeing the threads going out, but they are blocking forever. It's hard to fix because the URL class methods are preventing direct interaction with the IP stack, so I can't send the flags I want to debug it. I implemented threads so I could spawn the tests asynchronously, but some of them are dying so I have to bounce the client, which creates zombies dangling everywhere."

DEVELOPER WALKING BY (THE ANNOYER): "That's what you get for using Java. If you'd done it in C or C++, you wouldn't. . . ."

YOUR DEVELOPER: "You're such a language bigot."

THE BIGOT: "It's true."

YOUR DEVELOPER: "Well, I'm not backing out of it now!"

THE ANNOYER: "Then you'd better stop using that brain-damaged URL class. You can't explicitly set the parameters, like a timeout. It just blocks, and then you're dead. You don't know what the hell is happening."

YOU, THE MANAGER: (sigh) "So, what's the status. Is this a huge problem?"

YOUR DEVELOPER: "It could take a minute or a month to fix. It depends on how fast I can GROK it."

Your engineers and programmers are simply involved in the natural geek phenomenon of competitive wordplay. This is not some conspiracy of jargoneers to keep you in the dark; it is Geek Speak. Geek Speak is a form of shorthand, a rich patois that allows them to share very complex understandings of the systems they build in a language- and time-efficient manner. Despite its complexity, it is highly functional without any hidden agenda or false meaning. In LEVIATHAN(3), the authors observe the vastness and depth of the typical software project. In Geek Speak, developers can grasp and pass among themselves both the known and unknown aspects of the

LEVIATHAN(3). Furthermore, there is an unspoken competition among developers to both master and extend the vernacular in their particular dialect. Dialects, by the way, can be born and can die with single projects, or they can span decades of development. And like any competition, the result is either stronger, better-informed competitors, or tired, angry losers who accuse each other of cheating. You are the Geek Speak referee who sits back and lets the games continue, watching until violations become so blatant and egregious that you must cry "foul!"

The geek-aware manager has to hone her technique to know just when the dialectic is running in a circle. Remember that, while a kind of referee, you are still the SHAMELESS IGNORAMUS(14)—kind of like the postman refereeing professional football—and this competitive wordplay directly represents part of the dynamic of the Geek Order and, with your patience, it will ultimately work in your favor. If the interchange of ideas becomes stagnant (and even if you can't understand the language, the conveyance will make it clear), perhaps it's time for PEER PRESSURE(41) or, in severe cases in which the dialogue starts to resemble more of a blame game, DIRECT ACTION(19). If necessary, you can use DIRECT ACTION(19) as a way to implement quick PEER PRESSURE(41).

Remember that the value of TRIBAL LANGUAGE(17) doesn't always stop with the geeks. Larry Constantine notes, "Technical fields often have a rich interaction with ordinary vocabulary. The computer field has usurped many everyday words for narrow technical purposes. . . . It works the other way, too, of course. Technical terms enter the mainstream to the point that computer jargon now peppers conversations on the street."[1] Every time you complain about "crashing," "running out of memory," or "getting bandwidth," you have leveraged the tribe's language. Of course, you may be like an American trying to order a three-course dinner in Japanese using your pocket dictionary, but the native speakers can appreciate the effort, even though at other times they sneer. And when you hear that your software developer is about to make orphans out of all the children, don't call the cops and dive under your desk, this is Tribal Language at its most endearing.

Therefore:
Become a casual student of the dialect. Employ the help of one of your developers so that you can get at least a conversational knowledge of the current Geek Speak equivalent to learning how to say "please," "thank you," and

---

1. Constantine, Larry (1995). *Constantine on Peopleware*. Englewood Cliffs, NJ: Yourdon Press, 28.

"Where is the rest room?"—like you do when you visit countries in whose language you are not adept. To allay suspicions that you are trying to intrude too deeply, remember to remain a SHAMELESS IGNORAMUS(14). Finally, enjoy the feeling of being the SOCIAL JESTER(18) when you flub the usage or when you hopelessly screw up the terminology. Naturally, you'll have to be a decent punster or at least minimally clever with words, but it can earn you a lot of points to use even a few fragments of foreign speech in a clever manner. Just don't be TOO CLEVER BY HALF(15).

Poster promoting reading, showing a boy's smiling face and an open book, 1939.

18

Social Jester

. . . in management it seems that one must assume a persona of aloofness to maintain power. It is easier to exercise the unpleasant effects of your position with equanimity and emotional distance. This is a symptom of an authority-based management paradigm and the resulting compulsion to put aside the elements of human behavior that interfere with ascendance of the power structure.

As a manager, you feel you must remain somewhat aloof from your team members; yet, as a person with mortal needs, you still feel the need to have some sort of connection with your team. Despite the ever-present notions of hierarchical management and overbearing human resources directors who demand robot-like adherence to the mandated codes of behavior, this mode of behavior breaks down trust between leaders and their teams.

Work Projects Administration Poster Collection (Library of Congress); Posters of the WPA/Christopher DeNoon. Los Angeles: Wheatly Press, 1987, no. 199.

Elvis lives!

We agree with Rabelais: "For all your ills, I counsel laughter." This does not mean that you have to play Dr. Jekyll and Mr. Hyde in a misguided effort to build trust with your development team by cracking jokes one day and cracking heads the next. We're talking about the genuine ability to have a little fun at the expense of yourself by remembering that if you laugh at yourself first, it takes all the fun away from those who might laugh at you last. Unfortunately, if you truly do not have a sense of humor, of *self-deprecating* humor, this will be a challenge. In fact, we can think of nothing more difficult to cultivate than a sense of humor, yet never has a single characteristic been more vital to effectiveness in a leadership role as it is now in these fast-changing times.

We have seen many former colleagues move into management from the ranks of geekdom and become different people, almost as if it were an act of policy. One day we're joking, playing cards, and sharing frustrations, and suddenly our friend becomes "management." In one particular case, as far as we're concerned, it made her into a different species. It was as though, upon her promotion, she had been taken into the Star Chamber by the executive committee and let in on the sacred rites and manners of the Management Club. She no longer laughed at innocent jokes in meetings or in private, but first waited a beat or two, as if to measure the potential repercussions, and then carefully metered out her laugh to maintain a slight but critical distance between her and everyone else. Might this be happening to you?

———————————

Photograph by Robin Seidner, © 2000. All rights reserved.

With few exceptions, developers seem to rarely experience an uncontrollably, recklessly joyful laugh with their managers. It is as if the managers were to cop a giggle with the development staff, then they wouldn't be able to hold the staff to a deadline or dressing-down because most people don't enjoy failing the people that they enjoy and admire. We contend that building real human relationships with your developers may actually enhance your abilities to hone a sharp, high-performance development team.

Maybe you don't see yourself in our representation of the humor-hungry manager, and perhaps you still feel like you can have a beer and swap jokes with your developers. But what matters here is *their* perception of *you.* Dr. Thomas Gordon, in *Leader Effectiveness Training,* observed:

> Also, you are likely to observe some subtle (and some not so subtle) changes in the way the group members relate to you. Some who only weeks ago were your friends now appear to avoid you and exclude you from their lunch groups. Others may start showing signs of being afraid of you; they act defensively, more guarded in their conversations, less frank in sharing their problems.[1]

So, as you see, the chasm has widened from both sides. How do you reestablish your human credibility with these people who view you as strange and different? Gordon goes on in his book to document 14 coping mechanisms for group members in dealing with their managers, including such things as rebellion, hostility, cheating, tattling, submission, crying, and getting sick.[2] Although Gordon's analysis and reasoning are interesting, trying to find tactics to deal with each of these mechanisms would be exhausting and probably useless. Our medicine is laughter.

One company that exhibited many enlightened behaviors and policies had an annual employee appreciation day that included a karaoke setup during a free lunch served by managers. A steady line of managers made their way to the stage, singly and in groups, to expose themselves before noshing developers while warbling and screeching through top-40 and golden oldies. Those managers who were willing to go all out and add choreography were almost always leaders who had the most loyal followings among their people, and not because of their sensitive and artistic interpretations of *Proud Mary* and *All Shook Up.* Interestingly enough, even organized

---

1. Gordon, Thomas (1977). *Leadership Effectiveness Training.* New York: G. P. Putnam's Sons, 13.
2. Ibid., 15.

religion has been known to use this device—the leadership of the religious community puts on some sort of a display of utter foolishness as a reminder that even the most powerful among us is still human. Seeing a religious leader dressed up like a belly dancer makes that point exceptionally well.

The fact is that it's easier to relax and confide in someone who can make you laugh and yet still respect her. Relationships that encourage communication are very valuable to you as a leader, particularly when it leads to catching and solving problems before they become crippling to your projects and career.

> Therefore:
> Don't be afraid to be a little goofy, if it's in your nature. Don't always try to be right or believe that you should be. At social occasions, do something odd—tell a joke or, even better, *be* the joke. A little self-deprecation goes a long way toward breaking the ice.

This is a good way to play the SHAMELESS IGNORAMUS(14) and a clever way to light BACKFIRES(44) or get yourself some INOCULATION(28).

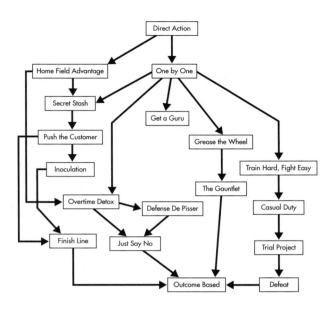

III

Strategic Patterns

The patterns in this section can be used to lay ground-work for future good in a current project and beyond. They focus on the care of the team itself as a unit that you plan on keeping together for a long time, creating a stable base in a turbulent world. In this section of the book, it becomes clear that attempting to manage on the level of unique individuals can be rife with conflict, con-fusion, and contagion. There are never any pat answers or nice problem-solution pairs. However, we believe that there are fundamental ways to frame your behavior that a manager can strategically rely upon to associate a team of individuals, each with their own ideas and agendas.

Nothing is more difficult for a leader than building a truly effective team, and once built, it is folly to lose the team. These patterns can help to unify, motivate, and defend your team so that they become and then remain a productive and effective unit.

Bottle of Congress Beer.

19

Direct Action

. . . the Temperance League strove to eradicate the use of alcohol in early twentieth-century United States by directly leveraging church, state, and the emotions of patriotism in the service of their mission. They also got down and dirty with instruments of destruction at times.

An advantage to direct action is that it doesn't require the cooperation of the authority to be effective. If they intervene to stop your action, you have a dramatic story; if they ignore you, you've followed your conscience and can continue following it further. Since the action in itself has a direct effect, it has a power and strength.[1]

Photograph by Theodore Horydczak, 1920; Library of Congress, Prints & Photographs Division, Theodore Horydczak Collection [LC-H822-T-1787-A-001 DLC].

1. From *The Nonviolence Web,* http://www.nonviolence.org/issues/action.htm.

◆◆◆

When projects are in trouble, following the prescribed process or falling back into authoritarian behavior can be attractive. Being true to the old ways provides a way to shelter your own actions from criticism. Rarely is anyone fired for following the rules! But to achieve success, if success is what you are *really* after, something riskier and more dramatic is usually necessary.

You are a leader with TOTAL COMMITMENT(2), but your projects may be in trouble. Times are tough and the temptation exists to fall back on known, proven coping patterns to get you through this time. Maybe a fresh Gantt chart, a dash of Total Quality Management, and a marathon meeting of the minds to hash out the problems, reach some sort of external consensus, and assign some accountability. No doubt that there is some company policy manual from a management class that can guide you. At least if your actions are questioned, you can refer to this higher authority and cover your posterior by having checked all the appropriate boxes.

You are in crisis mode here, and you've got to manage this mess somehow. After all, it's your butt on the line. Learning to stand up to power in the company is just part of the equation (TOTAL COMMITMENT(2)); leading your team effectively through tough times is another. It's not a mystery to you what the mechanisms for leading are, but where do you find the stuff within to be the right sort of leader, one who will be selected in The Manager Pool?

There are times when it is appropriate to put aside consideration, consensus, and concern for consequence and assert yourself as the leader of your team beyond the light touches provided by a GUIDING HAND(1). Sometimes that means taking direct responsibility for solving the problem. It means ignoring the prescribed processes, procedures, and methods that are employed by timid or career-sensitive managers and using your own brain to creatively assess and then to decisively act to create positive change. It means completely defying those in ultimate authority and risking termination. By doing so, you will lose your immunity to the consequences of failure. As it goes, *it's better to beg forgiveness than to ask permission.*

Learn from the temperance movement of the early twentieth century, which included many formerly timid women who moved beyond passing a few local laws to ban saloons to trying to solve the liquor problem in the United States. The Temperance League leveraged the churches for money and influence and ultimately leveraged the two-party system to drive their mission to the national prohibition of alcohol through a constitutional amendment. The forces used high-pressure political tactics, printed propaganda, and even the fervent anti-Kaiserism of World War I, to motivate politicians to pass the Eighteenth Amendment in 1919. The Amendment stood until 1933, when it was repealed during the years of the Great Depression because of the need for tax revenues. On occasion, temperance movement members took to axes, wrecking bars and smashing whiskey barrels in the streets. They refused to accept their place as demure and silent servants in a male-dominated society. Similar tactics are in use today in many ways:

> Our Job is not to be invited to coffee or to schmooze at a cocktail party. . . . Our Job is to make change happen as fast as possible and direct action works for that.[2]

Studying the temperance movement leaders may not be the most exciting historical foray for many, but by now you should know that driving one single project can be a lot like getting an entire country to give up its beer or to face the realities of a dreaded disease such as AIDS. Think of the isolation, the need to dampen outside meddling, the absolute necessity of maintaining morale throughout the stress, fear, and uncertainty. And always remember, you are the head of the movement; you must rally your team to be your union.

There is the obvious danger of being lured into the use of this pattern as a last resort—when it seems that all else has failed. In reality, when the project is in mortal danger, it is more likely that it is time to FALL ON THE GRENADE(51) or ABANDON SHIP(52). This scenario is described in an antipattern identified by Brown et al. in *AntiPatterns,* which describes how management can be deluded into taking DIRECT ACTION(19) when the time for its usefulness is actually long past:

> A few months into the project schedule it becomes clear to management that development must progress immediately. Impending project cancellation is the usual motivator. This situation is announced at an "all hands" Fire Drill launch meeting for development staff, during which management makes ambitious (or unrealistic) demands for software delivery. A typical example is a project that spends six months performing requirements analysis and planning, and then endeavors to design, implement, and demonstrate the software in less than four weeks.[3]

---

2. From Act Up (AIDS Coalition to Unleash Power) New York's web site, http://www.actupny.org/.
3. Brown, W. J., R. C. Malveau, W. H. Brown, et al. (1998). *AntiPatterns.* New York: Wiley and Sons, 263.

In this instance, DIRECT ACTION(19) may be the wrong play entirely. Depending on the context, it may mean simply standing up to denounce the proceedings. It might mean that when telling your team to forget the process, ditch the CASE[4] tools, and stop supporting anything not directly useful in producing the working code. Do not allow any member of the team to avoid technical responsibility in order to manage Microsoft Project charts or to operate on the safe fringe of the project in some lateral capacity. Make it clear that he is going to write code like everyone else or he is history. It may mean telling your own boss to stay away from your developers and you, or else! Once in a while, it may mean simply folding your arms and watching the whole stinking mess circle around and slide down the drain.

But you have the power, far more than you think, to profoundly affect the outcome of events. For the most part, many people in the corporate world are timid and fear to act directly and nakedly for all to see. This makes your will to do what is necessary all the more valuable and visible, whatever the outcome. You will be known as one who does not shirk in the heat of things.

There is always this eternal question from *Hamlet*:

> *To be, or not to be, that is the question.*
> *Whether 'tis nobler in the mind to suffer*
> *The slings and arrows of outrageous fortune,*
> *Or to take arms against a sea of troubles,*
> *And by opposing, end them.*[5]

To which he provided his own answer, but sadly did not take its heed:

> *. . . Now, whether it be*
> *Bestial oblivion, or some craven scruple*
> *Of thinking too precisely on th' event—*
> *A thought which, quarter'd, hath but one part wisdom*
> *And ever three parts coward—I do not know*
> *Why yet I live to say "This thing's to do,"*
> *Sith I have cause and strength and will and means*
> *To do 't.*[6]

---

4. CASE—Computer Aided Software Engineering.
5. Shakespeare, William (1980). *Hamlet* in *The Complete Works of William Shakespeare,* Third Ed., David Bevington, Ed. Glenview, IL: Scott, Foresman, and Co., *Hamlet,* Act III, Scene I.
6. Ibid., Act IV, Scene IV.

Therefore:

Seize fate by the scruff of the neck and force it *your way,* using only your conscience as your guide. Eschew political considerations, step off the manicured career path, and cut your own road. The time for negotiation and seeking permission is over. Do what *you* believe necessary to do to make things work. You know what to do. Now do it without fear. *Act!*

Malheur National Forest, Grant County, Oregon. Lumberjack measures "scales" log. He keeps a record of how many and what size logs are cut and estimates board feet that are cut. The best loggers worked on the basis of board feet produced rather than hours spent working.

20

Outcome Based

. . . software workers, like most others in America, are expected to be at their desks at least nine hours a day, including lunch, five days a week. And when the work demands it, which happens far too often, they are expected to be at their desks for even more hours. Managers are often comforted by knowing where their teams are, yet the creative acts or the duty of protracted concentration are often birthed at their own time and pace.

Developers require the flexibility to be personally expressive at certain times in the development process. However, the modern-day work force demands daily head counts, and some managers consciously count "face time"[1] in their appraisals of people's work.

Photograph by Russell Lee, 1942; Library of Congress, Prints & Photographs Division, FSA-OWI Collection [LC-USF346-073460-D DLC].

1. "Face time" is the amount of time your boss can see your face in the office. Some managers consider that you are working only when they can see you. If they only knew. . . .

Software creation requires the unique talents of developers to design, build, and reshape their products at an accelerated pace. But each developer has her own unique work pattern; some work quickly, others are deliberate, and a few will mumble incessantly, interrupting the drone only with agitated slaps to the monitor.

Yet in software production, developers are often viewed in somewhat the same manner as workers on an assembly line, or even as automatons. This misguided view has it that one developer will create the same code as any other developer given the same resources. Perhaps you even see your team as cogs in the machine that only need oiling and grinding to push them to their maximum limits of production. And, in fact, while many corporations continue to view their information technologists as factory workers, almost all the trappings of a traditional manufacturing environment are missing. There are no unions, and consistent overtime hours are not met with fatter paychecks at the end of the run. Software workers certainly don't strike, *although perhaps they should!*

With all that time spent glued to their glowing CPUs, consider, just for a moment, the productivity gains that could manifest in a world in which what matters is what developers do, not where and how long they sit. Start thinking of your software developers as valuable human beings who want to be appreciated for their inventive efforts and *outcomes,* rather than esteemed solely for amazing displays of intellectual stamina.

When you look at a work of art, do you judge its quality by the number of hours the artist took to create it or by its number of brush strokes? Let's hope not, or you are nerdy beyond redemption. Most people appreciate a work of art because of the mastery of craft and creative expression that is conveyed. We believe that many elements of software development should be viewed similarly. By recognizing the value of what your developers actually produce, contrary to the popular bean-counting notions of figuring lines of code or hours spent in the cube, you have an opportunity to *lead* your team to a successful outcome, rather than manage them to some level of mediocrity.

Forcing your developers into a rigid work schedule conveys the message that you do not trust them to do their jobs without your oversight. And this implicit presumption that your developers need to be managed like children (see FORTY WHACKS(16)) impels the outcome you most fear—massive project failure. Lost is the desire to create the best outcome or even examine the problems with any sense of adventure or personal investment.

You ostensibly hired them to build complicated systems for you that require highly specialized skill and knowledge. So what if they like to work after midnight loaded on Jolt cola or with a beer in hand? You hired them to produce effective software, not to sit in a chair, propped up in their cubes by 8:30 A.M. Remember you are paying for their brains, not their bottoms.

> Therefore:
> View the success of your employees by the quality of the work they produce, rather than by cumulative hours spent on each activity. Trust that your software developers' motivation for achievement and attainment will serve as an internal compass, keeping them from straying too far off course.

This pattern is expanded on explicitly in the pattern HOME FIELD ADVANTAGE(22) and managed by understanding different work styles and needs among your team members. Use a GUIDING HAND (1), learn how to GREASE THE WHEEL(30), and simply provide ENOUGH ROPE(45) or PEER PRESSURE(41) when necessary.

The eyes of the guru (lab coat optional), Paul Jordon, regional information adviser, region seven, Soil Conservation Service of the United States Resettlement Administration.

21

Get a Guru

. . . with a team in place and working on a project, the LEVIATHAN(3) *sinks deeper into the murk, and the* TRIBAL LANGUAGE(17) *quickly evolves. Even with a sound basis for your relationships with the team members, your ability to be a* SHAMELESS IGNORAMUS(14) *must be counterbalanced by some means of tapping into the technical well and retrieving a bucket or two of meaningful knowledge.*

Although you do not need to be and cannot be astute and erudite on all matters that exist within your domain, you nevertheless need to be able to take an in-depth reading of the ongoing activities in your domain. You need someone to help you.

Photograph by Arthur Rothstein, 1936; Library of Congress, Prints & Photographs Division, FSA-OWI Collection [LC-USF34-005273-EDLC].

Although we encourage managers to let go of their death grip on details concerning development (see GUIDING HAND(1) and SHAMELESS IGNORAMUS(14)), it remains necessary to take core samples, particularly when a problem that interweaves technology and business arises. For example, to improve a product release it is necessary for you to go to battle to extend the development schedule. To prevail in such a conflict, you have to appear as though you are so thoroughly knowledgeable and so convinced of the trade-offs that your logic is indisputable. However, the kind of study that such preparation may require can overtax your time and energy as described in SHAMELESS IGNORAMUS(14). Furthermore, if you are ill-prepared for such a meeting, you could be ambushed by someone who understands the jargon or the technology just enough to trip you up, or you could discredit yourself and your team if you are unable to satisfy those to whom you must make your case.

One approach to this, originating in a time-honored tradition from tribal cultures and modern ones alike, is to get a guru. Our definition of a guru is someone who has the respect of the development team and takes an active part in it, but who also has a knowledge and sympathy for the business side of things. This might be someone with whom you have worked for years, but it can also be someone who is less well known to you but has a true belief in what the team is doing and has a personal stake in seeing it executed well. If you can gain the confidence of such a person, she can become your coach, adviser, and interpreter, preparing materials and you for the DRAMA(4) that will be staged on your team's behalf.

A manager of our acquaintance, call him Roy, subscribed totally to the notion of SHAMELESS IGNORAMUS(14) and in casual conversation would reveal himself as ignorant of specific technical developments under his direction. He also acted unconcerned about any of the latest developments in the field. Despite this, in meetings in which he was required to report progress or argue for more resources, he would display an astonishing knowledge of the matters under discussion—and always with more technical depth than his peers and superiors in the room. The unseen part of this display was a longtime colleague named Spike, who had remained on the technical staff but who understood how valuable Roy was as her (yes, Spike is female) manager—able to block out interruptions, corporate misdirection, and meddling on behalf of all of his developers. Spike kept Roy in the loop on the really important things and would even accompany Roy to meetings as his technical expert if there were ever the possibility that a rival might bushwhack Roy or if an executive VP was going to prove stingy or hardheaded. Spike enjoyed the largess of Roy's complete trust and could even barter her value for a working schedule that was completely idiosyncratic. Spike's team understood and liked the special relationship that existed between her and Roy because it also allowed them a liberal range of movement in time and space so long as the work was done well and efficiently, in an OUTCOME BASED(20) manner. In a sense, Roy was a BLOW-HOLE(11) in his ability to mediate the conflicts between the business and technical sides of the project and to equalize the attendant pressures.

The guru is someone you can always rely on to translate for you and to act in your best interest, even when you don't understand the translation. The guru is a rare individual who is capable of understanding the technology as well as the larger business picture, but with a position and relationship that make her easily accepted by your developers. In other words, a developer herself, albeit one with a closer relationship to you that does not taint the relationship she has with her peers. You must rely on her for information, as well as for transferring business information to the development team.

Occasionally the guru will tell you that you're wrong and have to set you straight; this is the sanity check you desperately need to keep from becoming detached from the reality in the pits of development. The guru is also an ally in understanding the difference between truth and blowing smoke and in determining what the team or its individuals most need. *The guru is not a spy.*

In fact, the guru must have the highest integrity as viewed by both you and the developers. The guru is a two-way conduit and must be trusted completely by all with whom she interacts. The guru could actually replace you if she cared a whit about managing, but she's a technologist at heart and, quite frankly, doesn't want your headaches. But she may have worked for you for years and wants to help you keep your position so she can operate under the umbrella you provide her, free from the gridlock that the corporate processes and policies normally impose.

Great leaders always rely on advisers. US presidents and United Kingdom prime ministers and sultans of Brunei and generals and corporate kings all have staffs to supply them with knowledge on an as-needed basis. Even though we know that they cannot possibly really be so well rounded in all aspects of everything, we remain impressed when they show a long sliver of learning that penetrates to the heart of knowledge. Although you may be managing a team of only a dozen or six dozen rather than a nation, you should not be deprived of at least one trusted and savvy adviser who can make you look extraordinarily smart.

Therefore:
Establish a solid and trusting relationship with your guru, and defer to him on matters that drive deep into the technical world. Cultivate this relationship with

protections and leeway and accommodate any quirks in his way of working, as many such gurus are quirky personalities, indeed. Patiently study what he presents to you and make him proud of your abilities, for if you can please him, you will *rule* in the meeting room. Furthermore, have him join you to shore up any shaky parts in your understanding and let him glow in the spotlight so that your rivals and superiors will understand the depth of your operation.

This pattern can help ameliorate the pain caused by the phenomenon of TRIBAL LANGUAGE(17) and the essential need to be a SHAMELESS IGNORAMUS(14).

NY Giants baseball team,
1905.

22

Home Field Advantage

. . . there is a well-known phenomenon called the Home Field Advantage:
When a sports team is playing in their home city, they have the socially rein-
forcing advantage of an enthusiastic, supporting crowd. There is also a doc-
umented disadvantage related to a protesting home crowd, wherein team
performance is measurably degraded by an upsurge in aggressive penalties.[1]

In a high-technology climate of corporate raiding, outrageous compensation packages, diminished loyalty, and even arbitrary layoffs, effective management can sometimes mean attempting to derive the maximum benefit from a software developer in the shortest amount of time. Keeping a core team of reliable, conscientious, talented programmers seems impossible, but it can be the

Photographer unknown, Library of Congress, Prints and Photographs Division.

1. Leifer, Eric M. (1995). "Perverse effects of social support: Publics and performance in major league sports." *Social Forces,* 74, 81(41).

key difference in project achievement and your overall success as a manager and perhaps as a company.

Developers are accustomed to taking the blame for failed products, being treated with bizarre forms of disrespect by marketers, lampooned by the press, or generally being ignored except when there is an emergency. Stacks of books and reams of articles maligning the very nature and behavior "paradigms" of the software developer—they have been called spoiled, retentive, insane, and autistic—have been written. In fact, it was only a few years ago that pundits were predicting the demise of the programmer by the forces of automation. It's no secret that some managers would love to do anything to free themselves of the need to employ these people.

Many years ago when the Ada language was just coming into being as the lingua franca of software development by the United States Department of Defense, one of the authors was accosted by a manager of a defense-related development effort. "You lousy programmers. I can't wait until this Ada thing is finally defined because it's going to make all you creeps program alike. Then you won't be such wise guys." His astonishing faith in language development technology aside, this guy was probably expressing at least the momentary feelings of every manager by his forthright expression of contempt and mistrust.

In one instance, a product on which developers had slaved to cram a year's effort into four months failed to attract even a single customer. At a quarterly status meeting in which management presented the business's progress to all employees, the development team was astonished to learn that the reason the product hadn't sold was because they had not coded in the correct features (the ones they'd never been told about, of course). Naturally, marketing was making the presentation. The presenter, one slick weenie if ever there was one, managed to verbally intimate that the development team had been resistant and technically incapable of building what the market demanded. This would have been a time for managerial DIRECT ACTION(19) had the team's boss had the guts to create such SIGNIFICANT EVENTS(38). Instead, the developers sat and steamed over the injustice of being fingered as the culprits for a dead-end product. They hadn't conceived it, hadn't ever been permitted to speak with the customers, and hadn't been involved with the feature and schedule negotiations. All they had done was to put in twelve 80-hour weeks after being given the mission and to succeed in meeting an absolutely delusional schedule expectation. Now they were being completely trashed by their own marketing people in their own auditorium. No one cheered their efforts or attempted to buoy them up through the loss. There was no show of faith in them as the home team; instead, they were completely ridiculed. They were starting to feel like a bunch of losers, shamed while beer cups and soggy pretzels rained down on their heads.

It is fashionable in some quarters to use the designation *coach* instead of manager. Despite your true feelings about sports analogies, and perhaps being ever doubtful regarding this designation, your role should at least include being your team's best fan and cheerleader, especially when it comes under attack. Your job is to impart belief in the team's skills and judgment. And it must be a sincere belief that you convey by creating an environment of mutual trust, camaraderie, and *high expectations.* This is more than dishing out options that won't vest for years; rather, it is a public display of support. Your developers expect you to defend them against those who try to use them as scapegoats and against those who make easy targets of them because they usually don't have an opportunity to describe their travails. They could use pep talks at times that come from the heart, even when they screw up. Nothing raises a team like a loud cheer even when the team loses.

> Therefore:
> Treat every member of your team with the expectation that she will do a great job in a timely manner. Convey to your team your belief that you see them as professionals with special expertise and knowledge and that you are depending on them, as you would any professional. Like the rabid fan of a professional sports team, you expect that you have the talent on your side to pull down a win, but your enthusiastic support and belief in that talent is the means to a positive outcome.

Seabrook Farm, Cannery Workers, Bridgeton, New Jersey, June 1942.

23

Overtime Detox

. . . although it has been decades now since experts have decried the use of overtime as a panacea for bad planning, it continues to be the standard solution applied by managers in a crunch in project after project after project after project. . . .

Overtime, though it may plug short-term gaps and pull a manager's feet from the fire, remains the most abused and dangerous hammer in the management toolbox.

Photograph by John Collier, 1942; Voices from the Thirties, American Life Histories, 1936–1945. Library of Congress, Prints & Photographs Division, FSA-OWI Collection [LC-USF34-083260-C DLC].

We don't understand the passion for examining urine samples (see DEFENSE DE PISSER(24)) when the number one drug problem in the workplace is *overtime*. You can go to almost any company workplace at random and witness sleep-deprived zombie-like developers staring into the glare of monitors, unaware of whether they are awake or asleep or when they had slept last or even been out of the building. If you didn't know that their slow reactions, glazed eyes, and shuffling gaits were caused by overwork, you'd be running the drug-sniffing dogs through the building on a daily basis looking for Thorazine. Because it's caused by overtime, however, overtime that is encouraged and rewarded and honored, why worry about what it's doing to the quality of the work or the health of the developers? Who cares if they are beginning to look like crack addicts?

There *must* be something good about overtime. More than ever it has become part of the software development culture. Stories are legion of 60-, 80-, 100-plus-hour weeks, of people sleeping under their desks, of people taking their laptops with them into the restroom stall, of people never being offline for a moment. Working a 40-hour week is for the weak, the lame, the uninspired, and the ambitionless. If you get the reputation, as a developer, for working only your 40, people come to resent you, don't like teaming with you, and consider you unworthy of true geekdom. Even the geeks do it to themselves with all their posturing, so why in the world should you try and discourage what seems to be their natural tendency? Besides, you can exploit this very nature of the geek order to make up for your poor judgment in planning and staffing. Even in an unmitigated failure of a project, if your team's time charges are high enough, how could anyone blame you and them for not trying? It makes for some pretty good covering in a crisis.

We aren't just targeting unpaid overtime here. Some companies pay overtime, whether conditionally according to the value of a project or as a matter of policy, which can be a gold mine for the developers. In one company of our experience, developers learned that there would be a nine-month moratorium on raises, but not one of them was fazed. Owing to a policy of paying for overtime in excess of four hours a week, they simply hung around longer and gave themselves a raise. It was known as the OTGT—the Overtime Gravy Train. One wag even wrote a song about it:

> *Ridin' the OTGT*
> *Adds a hundred dollars a day.*
> *Don't wanna give me a raise, well,*
> *I'll just raise my own pay*
> *Ridin' the OTGT*

Gives me the money I need.
Though I gotta stay late every day,
I do just enough to succeed.
Ridin' the OTGT
Makes the boss think I care.
I still work *40 hours a week*
But gettin' paid for 50 seems fair.
Ridin' that OTGT
Ridin' that OTGT
Ridin' that OTGT.

In what has to be a most egregious use of overtime, one developer worked 54 hours per week for over 10 years! When he finally decided to buy a house, he applied for a mortgage somewhat larger than his base pay would qualify him to have. The lender balked, but when his company produced a letter on his behalf showing his decade of overtime, he was reconsidered and they classified his overtime pay as part of the base.

Quite often, it is the hours logged that count more than the accomplishments of the person working them. One colleague of ours refuses to work overtime so that he can be a good father to his son and true husband to his wife. In one particularly nasty crunch period, when all his teammates were working 60-plus-hour weeks, his boss pulled him aside for an attitude adjustment. Why wasn't he pulling his weight like the others? he was asked. "Well," he replied, "I get my job done in 40 hours. If you want, I can get my work done in 50 or 60 if that would be better, but it seems like an awful waste." The boss backed off, but our friend was not the beneficiary of his largesse come raise time. Some of his teammates admired him for sticking to his guns; after many weeks of this imbalance, each of them began to resent him, even as each wished he had the sheer courage to do the same thing. Either way, he had an "extra" 10 to 20 hours in a week to spend with his family and friends, time that was far more valuable than his passed-over raise and the congeniality of his peers. And that, for many of us, is reward enough.

You see, it's really up to *you* to end this ridiculous reliance on overtime, this culture of overtime, this false macho cult of overwork. Of course, we still have to make a case for its destructive effects.

One effect has already been mentioned—the inevitable resentment of coworkers toward those who refuse to participate, no matter how productive they are. A second is the total lack of any evidence that more hours equals more productivity.

Again, manufacturing theories and observations have been falsely applied to the creative work of software development.

And perhaps the most pernicious effect is the destruction of people's lives, introducing strains in relationships that are ultimately reflected in their work (see WHOLE PEOPLE(8)). It is no idle speculation that divorces are greater among engineers who work overtime habitually. In fact, we know of one manager who delighted in the high rate of failed marriages among his employees. "That means they have really gotten their priorities straight," he cackled with obvious glee. "Once the spouse is gone, there's no more competition for their time. In fact, a lot of them work even more hours to try and forget the troubles they've had." Admittedly, this guy was a really bad seed, but the sentiment lurks in many managers' hearts when they sense that their meaty bonuses may be in jeopardy.

Companies in the software industry are like alcoholics who keep falling off the overtime wagon. At the beginning of every project there are promises to avoid it, even as the schedule is being compressed by customer demands and compromised by marketing concessions. *This time will be different,* everyone promises. We have a solid plan in hand. We're smarter this time. Naturally, these promises are as hollow as those of a recidivist drunk with a pint of Old Crow in his back pocket. "Just for medicinal emergencies, I assure you." At the first sign of trouble, the cap is off, and that sucker is drained, followed by a fifth, a quart, and a case, until everyone passes out. The next morning in the project aftermath it all starts over. Back on the wagon, the team plans itself into another ridiculous schedule and the inevitable binge, all the while promising that that was the last time.

A formerly aggressive driver we know got a rather hefty speeding ticket some years back. The judge offered traffic school instead of a large fine and points against his driving license. He dreaded the idea of four evenings in a classroom for such a small offense, but it turned out that an important lesson was imparted in the second class. The instructor, a cheerful woman with an engaging teaching style who didn't take herself too seriously but took her work very seriously, asked if anyone in the class had ever rushed through traffic trying to make up for lost time. Perhaps they had left home too late or had not accounted for traffic or had tried to squeeze in too many errands. As she listed the many reasons one might find oneself pressed to drive a little faster and more recklessly, the hands went up until all of them were shown. She smiled, "Never try to compensate for your own bad planning by driving too fast. You endanger yourself and the safety of others. It's just not worth it."

Perhaps life and limb aren't directly threatened by overtime, but its corrosive effects can be just as deadly to quality of life. Are you seeing overtime habitually used as the panacea for bad planning? Is this habit accompanied by a fatalistic attitude that nothing can be done about schedules? You will feel extreme pressure to continue to conform to this view. We have seen edicts issued that forbid even the mention of scheduling in assessing project risks. The tone of these edicts coming from senior management sounds uncannily like those of a head of household who doesn't want the family's drunken or drug-addled member mentioned in public. Overtime is evidence of an illness, a disease of the organization. Paid or unpaid, planned or unplanned, it is a symptom of a refusal to acknowledge the true cost of development *up front.*

Therefore:

Oppose, through all means available to you, the temptation of overtime. Resist pressure to compress schedules without corresponding feature reduction (see Featurectomy (47)), staff increase, or both, or refuse to sign up for them if you know that the hidden schedule calls for massive overtime in the home stretch. Although short spurts of overtime are occasionally useful, they are useful only for solving *specific and discrete* problems.

Could reading the wrong periodical cost someone a job?

24

Defense De Pisser

. . . and one final thing. We'll need a sample. Please fill this vial at least to the line. The rest room is just across the hall. Please wash your hands thoroughly before and after donating. Thank you.

It's customary now to request that a potential employee provide a sample of his or her bodily fluids for your company's inspection. Seems pretty kinky to us, not to mention that you are engaging in what is really unreasonable search and seizure.

Urine tests, hair cuttings from the scalp, DNA screenings—why not give polygraphs or even submit prospective employees to some red-hot poker action, just to make sure they aren't hiding something? Obviously, if your company gives the whiz quiz, it doesn't really take to heart one of the fundamental protections of any free society. After all, this is a workplace, so why should you be restricted by these limp liberal notions of privacy and presumed innocence? Maybe you *like* the message your company sends as a drug-free workplace right at the onset.

That's nice. Intrusive, yes, violating, yes, but *drug-free, by God*. Very nice. It must be very encouraging to people whose skills are in short supply and who are pretty well educated and who probably haven't got time or inclination to be shooting dope that your company suspects them of drug abuse *up front* before it's even seen their work. Very smooth. Good message, that.

In the face of this fundamental mistrust, we don't really understand why any company stops just at drug testing. In reality, some of them don't. Many companies require personality testing upon hiring, and even search newsgroup archives for postings from potential employees, searching for possible insight into what is defined in the corporate manifesto as deviant behavior, say, political speech that strays into anarchic ravings or perhaps participation in a sexual fetish group such as alt.sex.binaries.plushtoys.squeak. For all we know, DNA material left on the complimentary coffee cup might be checked for chromosomal abnormalities following the interview. It's a slippery slope, folks, and it all starts with a little vial of pee-pee.

It would be one thing if the people you were interviewing were going to be conducting supertankers full of crude through Prince William Sound, flying Airbus 320s across the Atlantic, or rushing to accident scenes to extract victims with the Jaws of Life. One could argue that, in fact, they would be doing so, even though indirectly, through the software they will be designing and writing. But there is a big difference between immediate cause and effect situations (flying planes, performing surgery, driving huge trucks) and the long process of software development. If it weren't for the care and joy of all the testing and inspections and reviews that software is subject to (and we assume you do have a process for the development of software)—that is, if software was just written and then shot out into the world raw—then applying the standards of personal conduct for pilots and surgeons (who *aren't* drug screened, by the way) to software professionals seems more trouble than it's worth. To tell the truth, we are offended by it.

Many companies justify their drug-testing philosophy by claiming that just the possibility of urinalysis discourages applicants who might test positive. Is that necessarily a good thing? With the acute shortage of software engineers in the marketplace, do you want to be scaring away good talent just because they might indulge in weekend activities much like those you enjoyed during the Nixon administration?

How about those engineers who, given the wide selection of jobs available, do not apply on principle to any company that performs mandatory drug testing? Not only that, but some consulting firms also refuse to do business with companies that perform mandatory urinalysis testing. Consider which is the greater threat to your outstanding projects—lack of good engineers or stoned developers? When was the last time you had a project dashed because of your best programmer falling asleep at the keyboard from drug intoxication? When was the last time you ever heard of such a thing? Of course, the official line for this would be that the drug screening is working. Our advice on that score is to read OVERTIME DETOX(23).

Compared to the other pressures and stresses of the software development arena, illegal drug use doesn't even appear as a factor. Overtime, inadequate training, poor planning, lack of tools, unclear requirements, exhaustion, home/work conflicts, and more contribute to ill-fated projects, and, unfortunately, these are difficult things to remedy. How easy and wonderful, then, to be able to claim some level of purity by administering a little urine collection. "We are a drug-free workplace," your recruitment ads declare. Success, therefore, is guaranteed.

We don't intend on this becoming a howling vituperation against the War on Drugs in the United States or an advocacy for altered states of consciousness. We just think that drug testing, background checks on Internet usage, and other screenings not directly related to actual job competence belie a mentality in the management of a company that is based on paranoia and suspicion. It considers employees to be, by default, unstable, untrustworthy, unreliable, and unemployable. When you have gone to all the expense of recruiting candidates to your company, of rolling out the red carpet and making the case for you as the best employer in a world of many, asking someone to take a bottle into the small room and serve up a warm sample really destroys the mood. And what, really, is the reason for doing this at all?

As a manager, perhaps you don't believe there is much that you can do. We disagree with that assessment. Part of leadership is helping to guide company policy decisions based on evidence from the bottom up. As part of that bottom tier, we are asking you to start raising questions about your company's drug-testing policy. What is the rationale for this policy? What evidence was used to justify its implementation? What studies have been done since its beginning to validate its continuation? What message is the company sending to potential team members by subjecting them to such testing? What message is the company sending to current employees? Is recruitment being made tougher by such a policy? Is dedication to this policy something to justify regular testing of all employees? If not, why not? If random testing of existing employees is currently instituted, what have the results of this policy shown in terms of productivity and quality? What correlation in the world of software development between drug use and quality of software has ever been made?

You get the idea. We have the sneaking suspicion that your company's drug-testing policy, like all the others, was just a knee-jerk reaction to a temporal hysteria that has never been justified or proven. As engineers, our nature is such that we expect to see some compelling reasons to expel bladder brine into a jar. And don't take our word for it. *The Economist,* a conservative, pro-business weekly magazine of some repute, lends support for such a view.[1] "The attack on drugs has led to an erosion of civil liberties and an encroachment of the state that alarms liberals on America's right as well as old hippies of the left."[2]

> Therefore:
> Do your part to end this ridiculous ritual of urinating in a bottle or monitoring personal behavior in any manner by questioning the cost, effectiveness, and corporate reasoning behind the policy. Ask to see studies or other evidence that such programs actually result in better software, and measure such improvements, if any, against losses incurred through such testing.

If you are a recreational drug user yourself, you may consider taking a pass on this pattern as you may arouse needless suspicion and find a plastic cup on your desk in the morning.

---

1. *The Economist,* 28 July–3 August 2001 issue, special survey.
2. Ibid., section "A survey of illegal drugs," p. 12.

One of the great urinals of
Europe, in Amsterdam.

Toy gun fight, Boscobel, Wisconsin, 1939.

25

The Gauntlet

. . . slackers, goof-offs, glory hounds, whatever you want to call them, sadly it's inevitable that not every developer on a project is adding value. It can be difficult to figure exactly who is doing what and who is only pretending.

You sense that some developers just aren't carrying their part of the load, but you can't figure out how to tell who is putting up a smoke screen and who is actually getting the work done.

When you are managing a high-pressure development team, you can't risk disengaged employees who aren't doing their share. Unfortunately, most developers don't like to tattle on their own kind, and you may be at risk of missing the critical signs of team malfunction until a critical juncture is reached. You want to address

Photograph by John Vachon; Library of Congress, Prints & Photographs Division FSA-OWI Collection, [LC-USF33-T01-001539-M2 DLC].

the problem quietly, without calling in a grand jury or running your own private inquisition.

A developer known by one of the authors was difficult to work with because he was less concerned about turning out a good product than doing what he thought would garner him attention from any superior. It was hard to get agreement from him on how to proceed until he consulted his Special Edition VP Ouija Board. One developer turned to him during a meeting and shouted with unfettered frustration, "Look, if you want to smear Vaseline all over *your* lips and kiss Bishoff's butt, then do it without me." That was a sign. Yes, there are always signs. Sometimes, however, they are not so obvious.

The appearance of "busyness" can be a clue. Anyone who seems to spend a lot of time *coordinating* work rather than *doing* work may be playing a clever shell game by being involved in a lot of project aspects but actually contributing to none. Another potential sign is when someone seems inordinately fond of *raising* issues but never seems to be first in line to *resolve* them. In our view, anyone who is on a development team but is not doing technical work of some kind, is suspect. Everyone should have some skin in the game technically; that is, if anyone is able to totally escape doing work that can be either reviewed, inspected, or tested for value may not be doing anything of value at all. These, however, are just possible indicators, and it is essential that you not resort to asking individuals directly about who is and who is not pulling his or her weight. You shouldn't go on a fishing expedition without some solid evidence as to who the culprit is.

Fortunately, developers will conjure insidious ways to expose the problem members on the team, and you should really learn to detect them. Notice those who are not on the joke e-mail lists (of course, you may not be either), those who can't get any eye contact from his or her peers in a team meeting, and especially those who seem to be distanced from the team in a social manner. Remember that some developers are asocial but are treated in an amusing, playful way by their peers. These people aren't your problem.

Look out for the ones who cause all conversation to cease then they walk into a cube. Once you have an idea of who the troublemaker is, you can start a dialogue with his peers. As long as a developer is not doing the initial complaining, your chances of getting more information and soliciting solutions are much greater. Get them started, and they sing like canaries. But you have to be subtle, and you have to be careful. Injudicious use of information to leverage more privileged information may end up looking like some Machiavellian attempt to turn developers against their own. Unless you have clear indications that someone is not doing something useful on the project and is resented by the others, you could have the whole episode destroy whatever closeness and credibility you have.

Therefore:

Apply a legal-like standard of probable cause. Don't go looking for problems, but be sensitive to developers creating a psychological gauntlet for one of their own. If you catch something in the air, then start looking for more. If you reach a level of suspicion based on more than a single observation, then begin an investigation among the developers. You'll need corroboration from at least three members of the team to act decisively. If you are fair, diligent, and apply standards before you act, they may even start to respect your insight.

Examining the deterrence model.

Little girl pushing a carriage, Detroit, Michigan.

26

Push the Customer

. . . software development projects are hard to control, and predicting successful outcomes can be a fool's bet. They often morph in the strangest of ways with shifting requirements, creeping customer desires, new features, and ever-compressing development cycles.

Developers become angry and disgusted at working on "critical" projects that get canceled or mutated at the last minute, delaying or preventing a successful conclusion. They may have started to claim that things are "impossible" and can't be done, in an effort to find a way to disentangle from their absurd duties. You need to manage the chaos your customers are repeatedly trying to inflict upon you and your team.

Photograph by Arthur S. Siegel, 1942; Library of Congress, Prints & Photographs Division, FSA-OWI Collection [LC-USF34-110148-E DLC].

Albert Camus, in his rendering of the *Myth of Sisyphus,* notes that what makes Sisyphus such a tragic figure is that he was greatly aware of his punishment and his hopelessness of ever succeeding in his labor. It was precisely through this recognition of his own anguish that he found relief. This victory came from knowing, as he watched the rock descend yet again, that there was no hope for success when he began pushing the rock again from the bottom of the hill. His freedom came from knowing that his continuing torment was certain and that he was consciously refusing to hope!

A developer in a poorly managed high-tech world feels and behaves much like the tormented soul described by Camus—every working day is spent pushing the rock to the top of the hill only to see it roll back down, sometimes even back over him. Erratic decision-making, zigzags in policy, manic changes in features and schedules are rocks rolling over your developers' heads. You have your developers working hard on a project, designing, documenting, analyzing, and spending hours of their creative time to reach a deadline, typically not of their making. Cutting short their holidays or spending less time with their families and kids, they labor not to fall short of the finish line, only to see the project canceled by the clients at the last minute or changed so severely that most of their efforts end up in the bit bucket. Most customers will just push you around, because they can—if you let them.

To be an effective leader, you must protect your team from the preposterous conniving of many clients and customers who themselves carry stress and disorganization and who generally lack clarity in what they want from the project. Obtaining and communicating this kind of information is not always an obvious, linear assignment. In fact, it is a complex task to determine who and how to communicate the prescient information. Dave Olson, in *Exploiting Chaos: Cashing in on the Realities of Software Development,* notes that while chaos is normal in the process, there are boundaries to chaotic behavior that must be recognized and observed:

> Trees, for example, are very chaotic in their growth (including size, placement, and shape) but can be counted on to remain within particular ranges of sizes in particular growing conditions. The fact that these boundaries can sometimes be very precise is shown by the existence of the "tree line" on a mountain, that altitude above which no trees grow.[1]

Chaos is not the problem or the fear, but managing it is. Let your customers push *their* own rocks all over the mountain, below the tree line. Keep your develop-

---

1. Olson, Dave (1993). *Exploiting Chaos: Cashing in on the Realities of Software Development.* New York: Van Nostrand Reinhold, 35.

ers above, out of reach. As the keeper of this chaos, you can manage and set these particular parameters.

One developer tells the story of giving up the Christmas holiday with her three-year-old son and her visiting family. Unwilling to be viewed as the weak link in an already overdue project, she (among other developers on the project) continued working with terrible specs in an environment she had never programmed in before. After giving up the entire paid holiday, barely seeing her family, missing her son play with his new gifts, becoming exhausted, and feeling guilty for her choices, the project was delivered as the client had requested—on time. But, as the team had sardonically predicted, the project was canceled the first week of January, as the developers were flying home from the installation.

The manager was weak and her developers paid the penalty in a rather insulting way. As that manager sat at home, enjoying the spirit of the holidays, her developers were working. She should have pushed harder on that client to understand the full context of the effort or pushed the schedule back when it fell over the holidays. She lost the total respect of her team by not standing up for them as people and looked like a fool for not understanding the impending doom of the project. She should have known that there was only one customer and, even without an MBA, could have predicted what that meant for a 15-person development team. She was relieved of her management duties.

Unlike Sisyphus, you are not held under an eternal sentence of damnation. You can end the unending torment by pushing the rock of customer demand off the heads of your developers.

> Therefore:
> Tightly control your customer's expectations. Effective customer management is the key to ending an eternity of fruitless labor.

PUSH THE CUSTOMER(26) in conjunction with the judicious use of JUST SAY NO(29). Remember that software projects are like the LEVIATHAN(3). Give your development team the TOTAL COMMITMENT(2) that you will ensure that their efforts are not wasted. Kent Beck's book *eXtreme Programming eXplained*[2] covers some of this same territory with great insight and is highly, highly recommended.

---

2. Beck, Kent (2000). *eXtreme Programming eXplained.* Reading, MA: Addison-Wesley.

Finally, an ending with some significance.

27

Finish Line

. . . there is the need for an OUTCOME BASED(20) *system to better judge the accomplishments of a development team. However, for such a pattern to have meaning, one must first know what the desired outcome is.*

Software development projects have deadlines, but it is often rare for a team to clearly understand the vision for a project, let alone what the expected outcome *is*. With poorly defined goals and clients who throw in features at the last minute, developers may be unable to prioritize their tasks effectively to drive the project to success.

When running a race, pacing is critical. In longer races, such as a half-marathon or a marathon, the racer must know exactly where she is in relation to the finish line. Along the way, she tracks her splits and prepares for the final leg of the race, working to stay on pace. A half mile to two miles out, the racer pours on whatever energy is left, as she kicks it to the finish line. It is a carefully gauged effort that is successful only because the racer has primed herself to carry enough strength to get through that tape or down the chute. She knows that if she pushes too hard in the beginning, she will crash halfway through the race. She depends on the markers alerting her to the progress toward completion, and these inspire her to push to the finish.

Imagine what would happen to a field of runners if they had no idea how long the race was when the starting gun was fired. Some would sprint off the line hoping for a 5K race, others would attempt to pace themselves, preparing for the long haul, and the rest would probably take a few steps and decide to bag it. Adrenaline would be flowing and chaos would ensue. As one runner friend of ours stated when presented with this scenario, "ridiculous." Yet, in software development projects, this is precisely the model that we work under. Often, it is not even clear when a project has begun. When a team is told that the finish is near, a project revision plucks them up and dumps them back at the start; features change, management changes, or technical difficulties construct formidable barriers to completion. Even the most straightforward of development events can mutate into a steeplechase course of indeterminate length.

At the highest level, it is not uncommon to exclude the developers from discussions of vision and purpose for the software they are being asked to create. And little opportunity is afforded to provide input into how it can best be built. Not that many developers want to sit through these kinds of meetings, but there are experts who should be pulled in at the appropriate time during the definition process to help work on establishing the major markers along the path. Unfortunately, the project frameworks usually presented are vague at best, and the team is often left to its own devices to apply the technical decisions. But in a world in which the software engineers are often forbidden from even speaking to the customers about the product, or otherwise completely denied access to them, what is delivered is what was defined.

Realize that the majority of our understanding for the project work is translated by you, the manager, who often lacks the basic TRIBAL LANGUAGE(17) to convey the problem usefully. Perhaps you're not even sure what is supposed to be done—this makes a useful translation nearly impossible. If you can manage to establish clearly defined measures of achievement with your team that are in agreement with the customer's goals, then you have defined what it takes to get the job done. Once it is known where the finish line is and what the intermediate goals are, the team can pace itself, and it is much less likely to get derailed by laying back too long or kicking too early.

Another cause for project confusion is the poorly focused client. Because the manager has failed to clearly define the project from the beginning, clients feel comfortable throwing in features at the last second (PUSH THE CUSTOMER(26)). When the expectation and the project scope change midstream, developers lose the comfort of knowing what the ultimate goals are for the project and are left to guess. Furthermore, the addition of features at the end of a project, not accounted for, can often lead to nasty code that will cost more to fix than defining a new revision of the product to handle the changes. The finish line has been moved, the pacing has been totally thrown off, prioritizing is impossible, and confusion abounds.

When a project is clearly defined, and the manager enforces the original goals and intentions of the project, the manager ultimately forces the client's hand: Either cancel the project and throw out all of your efforts, or fund a revision. For many clients, if handled properly, this is a no-brainer. When presented with the facts, they will stick with their baseline product and quickly schedule revisions if their features are important enough. By getting a solid project out on time, with a reasonable versioning schedule, everyone smells better.

Therefore:
Clearly define the measurable outcomes for your project with the customer and the team, and ensure that they are simply stated and clear. Bring in technical expertise early to help define as much of the high-level technical framework as is reasonable. Stay true to your goals. Defer late requirements to subsequent revisions.

PUSH THE CUSTOMER(26) when necessary to set the markers to the FINISH LINE(27). Apply FEATURECTOMY(47) as needed to keep the pace up and consistent, and JUST SAY NO(29) when changes will endanger the process.

Marathon finish line, Huntsville, Alabama, 1978.

Author's private photograph; photographer unknown.

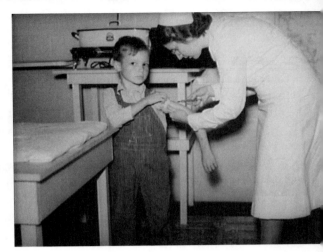

Inoculation for typhoid in the clinic at Irwinville Farms, Georgia, May 1938.

28

Inoculation

. . . inoculation against a disease, more commonly called vaccination, is when a weakened form of the disease is injected into the body. The body creates antibodies to fight against the invasive disease. Then, when a person is exposed to the disease, the proper antibodies already exist to destroy those particular bugs.

A bad bout with the wrong person in your project life span at the wrong time can wreak havoc with your projects, permanently disable the health of your career, or undermine your operational confidence and leadership abilities. It is hard to know who will cause problems in the execution of your project plans. If you or your team is expected to have contact with elements alien to the environment or culture, a project illness could result.

Photograph by John Vachon, 1938; Library of Congress, Prints & Photographs Division, FSA-OWI Collection [LC-USF34-008463-D DLC].

There are many occasions when a project will be cross-functional in some manner, often expanding outside your department or even your company. There may be personalities directly working with your team that you have never met until the day the project begins. Unlike engineering teams that often grow to a state of homogeneity because of TRIBAL LANGUAGE(17), projects that draw from diverse areas of the company or across companies bring their own rules and language. The new wave of cross-corporate alliances brings together entirely diverse cultures that may not even have a common point of view. For example . . .

The kickoff meeting for a half-million-dollar project was a disaster. Two teams from two very different companies would be working together to deliver on a wholly new concept about delivering rock concerts over the Internet. The cowboy startup, Blabstuff.com from the Valley, would be working with Cable General to bring kids in Middle America the content they demanded from new media sources. The two companies couldn't be more different in temperament and longevity, but the company principals had met at a broadcasting event and felt they could make this alliance work.

A lot of cash and resources were being put forth, and Dan Stalworth was given his first major project. Dan had been with Cable General for years and had finally progressed from software engineer to technical manager. This was his big break in the company, yet it didn't seem like it was going to be easy. It had taken him weeks to bring a first meeting to fruition, which worried him because he had already laid out the project milestones and knew that this project would take every bit of a year. Max Smith from Blabstuff.com was notoriously hard to get on the phone, let alone work with to arrange a geographically disparate meeting with the right people in attendance. The legal agreements kept getting changed at the last minute, and the whole meeting had finally come together only with the help of a thread of crazy e-mails.

The Cable General team had been sitting in the meeting room waiting for more than an hour—patiently, with their notebooks open. Dan looked fresh in his chinos, pressed white shirt, and blue blazer. He had placed the carefully organized and printed agendas at each seat and carefully reviewed his favorite management book about running a meeting for success just prior to work that morning. But when the Blabstuff team wandered through the door, it was obvious that the management gurus had missed something. Max, the Blabstuff lead, appeared to be either hooked to the gills on cocaine or hadn't slept in a week. He incoherently tried to introduce himself and never stopped babbling for the duration of the meeting. His cohorts, each and every one dressed in black, had no clue why they were even in attendance. The Cable General engineers watched with amusement, ate their free lunches, and then excused themselves one by one throughout the day.

Four hours later the project was already tail spinning to failure, as the two teams could not even agree on one sentence, which defined the ultimate goal of their effort. The initial impressions that the two teams developed of each other never corrected themselves; in particular, Cable General never took the technologists from Blabstuff seriously. In fact, they avoided any contact with them judiciously unless they were in the mood for a trip to the San Francisco Bay area. And Blabstuff.com couldn't even be relied upon to show up for meetings of their own design. On one occasion, Dan called before he flew to the Bay Area for a meeting and called to confirm before he got in the cab, yet the meeting with Max was canceled 10 minutes after he arrived because of a scheduling conflict.

Throughout the life of the project, any discussions continued to be hashed to death, literally. Not one solid idea ever made it off the table. One year and a half-million bucks later, a weak result was presented but canned by Cable General leadership before it went to the public. Dan spent the next six months covering his butt, and Blabstuff.com, without having delivered much of anything, went public in one of the most successful public offerings ever.

But strangely enough, Dan and Max grew to be friends during the travails of the year, and over coffee together a couple of months later in an informal postmortem they had a frank discussion about what went wrong. It turns out Blabstuff.com had never been in a position to deliver on the original terms of the agreement, as the CEO had overblown the capabilities of the company. Max and his team had been seriously oversubscribed, were working nonstop overtime (see OVERTIME DETOX (23)) ever since, and had been thrashing out of fear and confusion. Dan couldn't help thinking to himself that if he had taken the time to get to know Max early on and had asked the right questions instead of pressing his shirts or reading his useless management books, the project might have had a chance of success.

The human elements that ultimately define the success or failure of a project cannot be ignored. Dan had caught the disease of thinking a project was Gantt Charts, PERT Charts, milestones, and the almighty Measure of Success (MOS). Had he taken the time early on to personally align with the other members of leadership and develop a synergy between the teams, they could have spent a year working on the project itself rather than trying to recover from one bad day.

Cowboy filling syringe with blackleg serum, Quarter Circle U Ranch roundup, Montana, June 1939.

Therefore:
Expose yourself to the many personalities that will be involved in your project. Expose your team as well. Take steps early on to understand the personalities you will be working with and find some common ground, both substantially and stylistically. This will prevent you from being blindsided at a point in the project life cycle when recovery is more difficult.

This pattern is a partner with BACKFIRES(44) as a preventive measure. CULTURAL COMPETENCE(9) can be a blessed arrow in your quiver when tipped with the right knowledge for successful INOCULATION(28).

Photograph by Arthur Rothstein, 1939; Library of Congress, Prints & Photographs Division, FSA-OWI Collection [LC-USF33-003241-M1 DLC].

Striking field workers at the King Farm near Morrisville, Pennsylvania, 1938. These boys were very active in organizing the strike.

29

Just Say No

. . . the failure of the "Just Say No" campaign has been attributed to what some consider to be a faulty assumption—that kids are constantly in the position of having to say no. In fact, the widespread fuss may have created a climate that caused kids to believe that everyone was doing drugs, and so they became gripped with the fear of having to differentiate themselves from their peers.

Unfocused customers result in unfocused products, and they are no fun for the end users who are ultimately saddled with the ridiculous, misguided results. Your efforts and the efforts of your development team could be completely wasted. And while the project money may have seemed nice to the budget hawks, it can cost your team more than it earned in developer

Photograph by John Vachon, 1938; Library of Congress, Prints & Photographs Division, FSA-OWI Collection [LC-USF34-008558-D DLC].

frustration and disenfranchisement. Laid to waste are your best efforts of lead-ing with TOTAL COMMITMENT(2).

You are constantly dealing with clients, who lose focus, who change schedules and scope, and who add features about as often as they go to the bathroom after a three-martini lunch. But, hey, let's face it, they've got all the money and you need it. If you, as a manager of a software development team, start saying "no" to these out-rageously confused clients, you're going to get a bad reputation among your peers. Besides, any other manager would take these clients without hesitation if it means money flowing in the door!

Unfortunately, all of us can be like teenagers, who see any condition that differ-entiates them from their peers as one to be avoided, no matter what the costs. Know-ing that smoking cigarettes causes cancer isn't enough to dissuade an easily pressured teenager; knowing that your project will fail with the mucking and inter-ference of an uncontrollable client isn't enough to prevent a needy manager from taking the work anyway.

Some experts in the field of drug-abuse resistance education think a bit more broadly than the "Just Say No" contingent. They believe that we should go beyond utterances of "no" and instead dispense accurate information to kids. That is, correct teen perceptions about who is actually using drugs in an effort to teach them that it is indeed "normal" to say no and that, despite the howling and panicked wailing of the politicians, everyone is not "doing it."

A study at Penn State[1] indicated that most seventh graders believed that a majority of kids were using drugs and alcohol, but the same study indicated that actually less than five percent of those students actually were. It appeared that these kids had developed faulty impressions about the prevalence of drug use. Once they were taught that there was not an overwhelming menace that needed constant resis-tance, they actually were able to utter an informed "no" without fear of ostracism and martyrdom. In fact, saying "no" would not differentiate them from the wide majority of their peers.

Managers need to make informed decisions that take into account the impact that their choices have on their software developers. An effective manager says *no* to misguided ventures; to continue to expose your developers to fruitless ventures ulti-

---

1. Graham, John. Drug Abuse Prevention: Beyond "Just Say No." Online at http://www.hhdev.psu.edu/research/norm.htm.

mately results in your own massive failure, even if in the short term you can trumpet the revenue you *might* bring in. You will lose the intellectual capital that was yours by losing your developers to smarter managers and smarter companies. After all, smart managers are not wasting the precious time of their developers with disordered projects. Don't believe the propaganda that *anyone* would take an ill-defined project.

To say no with confidence, remember that your developers have resources that are expensive and hard to replace—brains and intellectual stamina. Many developers endeavor to do things in their lives that will be respected and useful to others, and a disorganized project that leads to months of waste is very hard to swallow. They like to be seen as creative souls effecting far-reaching results, and it is quite annoying to see an effort being doomed from the beginning by a project that is poorly conceived and therefore sloppily executed. It's particularly galling because it is the developers who tend to take the brunt of the blame for these failures from the marketeers in the front office.

One software programmer we know, after many productive years of software development, refers most contentedly to a graphical display that is used by pilots to land safely in adverse weather—he contributed the rendering routine for *one line* that shows the movement of a gust front! But the value of that line is considerable. The time spent on that project is worthwhile, even today.

We agree wholeheartedly with Thomas A. Stewart in his refreshing business book *Intellectual Capital.* He identifies quite succinctly how little else supersedes the love of craft:

> You hang your hat at Citicorp, Disney, or Whirlpool. The question is where is your heart? Increasingly, workers offer their first, deepest loyalty to their professions and communities of practice rather than to their employers. In these days of free agency, athletes think of their value in terms of being linebackers or shortstops, rather than being Bears or Cubs. For obvious reasons, the same is true of knowledge workers, a fact that underscores the fundamental conundrum of human capital: *People can be rented, but not owned.*[2]

An effective leader should be able to read the warning signs of a disorganized client by asking him to define the goal of his project in one sentence. After all, a client should know what it is that he wants to build. He should have a goal in mind that

---

2. Stewart, Thomas A. (1997). *Intellectual Capital.* New York: Doubleday/Currency, 100.

you can help him find a path to defining. If he can't even do that, or if he bathes his clouded vision in technobabble, you had better think twice about taking the project.

> Therefore:
> Be prepared to turn down lucrative deals if your client lacks clarity of vision. One cannot define a project and a plan that will lead to success without a baseline of reliable information. If your client can't provide a modicum of incisiveness and you can't seem to squeeze it out of him to your satisfaction, then say no to this project.

This pattern is closely related to many high-level patterns, such as TOTAL COMMITMENT(2), that help a manager start to think about her software developers as actual human beings with valuable intellectual capital. This is also a low-level practical pattern that reminds the smart manager to PUSH THE CUSTOMER(26) and not to sink his team with lousy work that will inevitably require him to ABANDON SHIP(52) or to FALL ON THE GRENADE(51) (which is sometimes the ultimate form of creating BACKFIRES(44)). Maybe a radical FEATURECTOMY(47) will do the trick.

Day laborer pushing wheel onto tractor, large farm near Ralls, Texas.

30

Grease the Wheel

. . . this agricultural worker knows all about squeaky wheels. The work is hard enough without a machine failure in the middle of the harvest.

You have a grouch on your team that seems to find fault with all of your ideas. Every time you open your mouth to frame, update, or schedule items relative to your project, this person grouses. The individual isn't overtly destructive but distracts from the core focus of the meetings. The rest of your team seems to enjoy your squirming as you defend yourself repeatedly against attack—almost as if this is just a quick game of foosball and you're what's getting whacked around.

Photograph by Lee Russell, 1939. Library of Congress, Prints & Photographs Division, FSA-OWI Collection [LC-USF33-012221-M4 DLC].

129

It may seem odd, but you like this person most of the time, and it seems like the rest of your team does, too. It doesn't make sense to fire her—she always pitches in and meets her goals in a timely and efficient manner. If anything, she performs beyond expectations. You also don't want to offend her or publicly embarrass her by a slight with sarcasm or innuendo—you've seen that backfire enough times.

Sit back in your next meeting as Josephine Whiner launches into another discourse about your failures, her pressure, and the perennial list of company shortcomings, and consider this an opportunity to capitalize on. Not only can you gratify the motormouth, but you may walk away from this meeting knowing that you have successfully focused this person's energy. Turn complaint into vital information that has the potential to move and shake your team or dispel it as fumes vented from a chronic gasbag.

Consider the forces that are at work in this scenario. Why does this geek keep mercilessly lashing out at you? There are several possibilities, and the authors have seen all of them at one meeting or another:

- ◆ You really are screwing up, and she is trying to help you out, but she lacks the basic skills of negotiation to convey the message effectively.

- ◆ She sees herself as a devil's advocate who is facilitating the process.

- ◆ She is hungry for recognition.

- ◆ She is a hopeless self-aggrandizer.

- ◆ She is a needy, pathological victim.

- ◆ The geeks find it hysterically funny to watch when you defend the schemes of the company.

The bedrock of the solution is to listen, observe, recognize the real motivation, and use what you have learned about this person—what she is trying to convey immediately and productively. What needs is this person trying to satisfy? Is she bored or right on the money? By determining what factors are really at play with this individual—and you don't need pop psychology to teach you how to shut your mouth and listen attentively for a few minutes—you will be able to use your study time to greater advantage.

Listen to the person and let her spool herself out—let the squeaky wheel grease itself. While she is whacking you from this side of the room to the other, meditate on the following quote from Sun Tzu's *Teachings on the Art of War:* "Let your fortress appear to be empty."[1]

Take a moment and avoid the temptation to defend yourself or your company, so that you may focus the attention away from your power and allow the attack to go unchallenged. A tendency toward pathological power will not serve you; as a manager, your job is simply to learn how to focus your team's energy toward the goal of getting the job done well, on time, and as much within budget as humanly possible. When you have really listened, heard, and recorded the concerns of your team member, be glad that she brought up her concerns. Now is the time to try and turn dross into gold.

> Therefore:
> Ask the person to document her concerns and present them to you and the group at large when you can address them without distraction. She just might have something that is helpful, and you'll have benefited from her insight. Or, she might just let the matter drop, and you will have become a fortress not worthy of attack. Either way, you move forward.

Documenting concerns about the project will feel an awful lot like work, and documentation is about the last thing that any self-respecting software engineer wants to do more of. Preventive measures to stop a potential squeaky wheel are to get INOCULATION(28) and to set BACKFIRES(44) where necessary. The incidences will become part of the TRIBAL LANGUAGE(17), and your ability to handle the squeaky wheel will find its place within it. However, this might be a preface to handing someone ENOUGH ROPE(45), after which the problem will correct itself, or you'll find that it's time to pluck some ROTTEN FRUIT(46).

---

1. Cleary, Thomas (1994). *The Human Element.* Boston, MA: Shambhala Publications, 128.

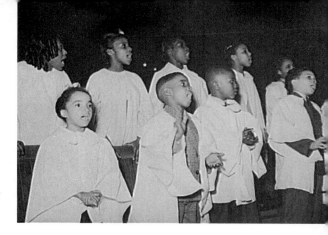

Children's Choir of Pentecostal Church, Chicago, Illinois.

31

One by One

. . . to produce beautiful music, each voice in the choir must lend its own particular quality to create one whole, integrated sound.

Large, chronically scheduled meetings are to programmers just another interface to be negotiated. It means recounting and deconstructing all of the superfluous interactions that led up to this moment. Putting a bunch of developers together in a room and asking them to defend themselves in front of their peers, especially if they are having trouble, undermines your HOME FIELD ADVANTAGE(22).

Some software managers like team meetings, and lots of them. After all, you want to encourage your team members to share their ideas, and you want to provide

Photograph by Lee Russell, 1941; Library of Congress, Prints & Photographs Division, FSA-OWI Collection [LC-USF34-038782-D DLC].

them with opportunities to collaborate and brainstorm. You are also convinced that frequent meetings, wherever and whenever they can be scheduled, allow feelings of shared values and commitment to the project vision to emerge. All attendees are encouraged to provide a detailed account of their efforts and describe how they fit into the big picture.

These meetings can be quickly derailed and result in convoluted, confused accountings that too often seem to serve as defensive maneuvers, boasting sessions, or painfully detailed anecdotes of the events that led up to the latest problem or success. These descriptions become particularly distressing if the developer has fallen on hard times either personally or professionally—he will derive some convoluted scenario that seems to provide blame for someone or something else for the limited progress. Before you think it's time to GREASE THE WHEEL(30) or hand out ENOUGH ROPE(45), consider a change to your meeting mania.

One software manager we know never seemed to be able to achieve the collaborative success she was hoping for in her meetings. In fact, by the end of the day she was usually reaching for a Valium, and the team was more cynical and sarcastic than ever. One member of the team had health problems and would detail each test and diagnosis, complete with his most recent blood sugar values. Another member detailed every frustrating phone call she had with the client that week—word for word. The low-level engineers in the crowd would mumble unintelligible phrases in TRIBAL LANGUAGE(17), hoping that the manager would just skip to the next victim.

The result was not collaborative problem solving but a brand of geek humiliation. The nature of the geek is not one of refined presentation skills that cut to the crux of the matter. In fact, engineers are often unaware of the point of their message—rambling on with long nonsensical diatribes projected under the guise of adding to the TRIBAL LANGUAGE(17). At some level, they sense that they are being misunderstood but feel powerless to stem the flow of words.

This is because programmers are taught to consider every remote possibility in their drive to understand complicated system interactions, their LEVIATHAN(3). Therefore, they need to explain every event leading up to the conclusion of their story so that there is a logical flow (at least in their minds) with a predictable outcome. This is, after all, what you pay them for.

Alan Cooper, in *The Inmates Are Running the Asylum,* refers to programmers as *Homo Logicus* in his typically sarcastic, yet, in this case, accurate view:

Normal humans are quite content not to know how something works, even though they use it and depend on it in their everyday lives. They see implementation model interfaces as imposing an unnecessary burden of understanding on them. Programmers find such attitudes inscrutable.

. . . In the world of software—which is the world of precisely articulated propositions—enormously remote possibilities are issues that cannot be ignored.[1]

Large team meetings are often boring and draining. When the project manager of a software development team throws a meeting, it should be focused on removing the barriers to a successful project—resources, programming problems, or the like. It should not be about interrupting the flow of work, just to see how everyone's getting along these days. Ask yourself this question, "What does this have to do with a successful product release?"

You are inundated with trendy management models that promise you a silver bullet to end your problems. You probably read in some management book or pop psychology book about group dynamics that involve getting your team in a room and letting them thrash as a way of generating new ideas and, ultimately, creating coherent group thinking. Most management books refer to this type of interaction as *collaboration*. The *American Heritage Dictionary*[2] provides a dual definition for collaboration that is very enlightening:

1. To work together, especially in a joint intellectual effort.

2. To cooperate treasonably, as with an enemy occupation force in one's country.

Managers may talk about collaboration, but your programmers are simply cooperating with you so that they can return to their cubes and can get the job done.

Collaboration (definition number one, anyway) is absolutely key to the creative process of development, and it most often occurs for developers in PUBLIC SPACE(57) or in pairs in front of a white board. In fact, collaboration occurs despite what seems like a plot by management to waste precious time with useless process definition meetings. Creative harmony occurs when we are afforded the opportunity to express our independent nature, no matter how it defies the undifferentiated solutions provided by the modern day guidebooks of the management stratum.

---

1. Cooper, Alan (1999). *The Inmates Are Running the Asylum: Why High Tech Products Drive Us Crazy and How to Restore the Sanity.* Indianapolis: Sams, 99.
2. American Heritage Dictionaries, Eds. (2000). *The American Heritage Dictionary of the English Language,* Fourth Ed.; Joseph P. Pickett (Introduction). Boston, MA: Houghton Mifflin.

Christopher Alexander, in his pattern "Mosaic of Subcultures,"[3] describes the problem of cities killing off the diversity of lifestyles and the resulting arrest of individual character:

> But euphemisms do little to disguise the fact that people who do things because that's the way to get along with others, instead of doing what they believe in, do it because it avoids coming to terms with their own self, and standing on it, and confronting others with it. It is easy to defend this weakness of character on the grounds of expediency. But however many excuses are made for it, in the end weakness of character destroys a person; no one weak in character can love himself. The self-hate that it creates is not a condition in which a persona can become whole.[4]

Asking your developers to buy in to your latest management process proposition is asking them to discard the demands of their own creative, independent motivations.

The next time you listen to beautiful music, remember that it relies on the particular value that each voice brings. Some may be stronger or richer, but every voice contributes to the whole sense of harmony. Your software developers may each sing to a different tune, but without them, you have no voice.

Therefore:
Geeks respond better to individual attention, to small, specifically focused groups, or to informal opportunities to have fun and knock around a tough problem. Small groups where hubris and humiliation *are* put aside will engender good feelings, better ideas, and great collaboration. Rather than having large round-the-table updates, walk around, and engage small groups of engineers in a natural setting.

A TRIAL PROJECT(33) or CASUAL DUTY(36) can help you get to know your developers individually without too much pressure.

---

3. Alexander, Christopher (1975). *A Pattern Language*. New York: Oxford University Press, 42.
4. Ibid., 45.

Fort Belvoir, Virginia, 1941.

32

Train Hard, Fight Easy

. . . .projects bumble, stumble, and sometimes crumble as teams fail to organize themselves under pressure. Although unorthodox in today's high-speed and high-pressure development world, preparation can make all the difference.

When teams are thrown together and then presented with a project without first establishing team mentality or shared skills, knowledge, or vocabulary, everyone learns "on the job," by trial and error. Team dynamics are left to work themselves out in the pressure cooker of the project.

Schedules determine everything. Once you're committed to a delivery, taking time out to build team spirit and cohesion is not acceptable to anyone involved. Yet

Photograph by Royden Dixon. Library of Congress, Prints & Photographs Division, FSA-OWI Collection [LC-USF34-014509-D DLC].

we know quite well that good teams take time to form. The cost of whatever training is required will be exacted, whether at the hidden expense of the project or at the explicit expense of training costs. In any project, members tend to try to self-educate, resulting in a lack of common culture or vocabulary. Additionally, with schedule pressures, internal competition, egotism, and fear, members may degenerate into one-upmanship, expressed often by hoarding vital information from team members that makes them look especially good to management.

You try to make do with what you've got, but there are obvious benefits to training. Training flattens the knowledge distribution curve. Training sessions themselves can reduce formality and barriers among team members as they collaborate on exercises and discover each other to be more or less knowledgeable in other areas than they are. Common vocabularies, essential to teams, are formed in training environments as the participants adopt the patois of new technology. Training can also be psychologically restful, as the developer is provided a break from the daily grind, giving the corporation a streak of goodwill.

Unfortunately, training is expensive, and training costs stand out, because they are usually marked separately from development costs in the budget. Nevertheless, it's hard to argue against training being worthwhile. The question is, are you willing to bite the bullet up front and fund the necessary training for the team, exposing yourself as potentially too generous and pampering? Or, would you rather do what many managers choose to do by hiding the explicit cost of training in the project budget as your developers educate themselves on an as-needed basis under the extreme pressure of deadlines? Think about which will be more effective in the long run and which will yield the higher quality of knowledge.

Training has another requirement to be truly effective. It's best to train teams, as much as possible, together in the same classes. Early training given to a team as a whole does far more than just educate the individuals—it helps to really gel the team in all the right ways, especially in the development of a cohesive, intelligible TRIBAL LANGUAGE(17).

It's not hard to see why. Training classes are neutral ground, usually relaxed, and with drinks and munchies that further reduce the formality. If the subject is new to everyone, then the übergeeks and the mere mortals, for the moment at least, occupy level ground. New champions may emerge and new respect distributed as different individuals master the new skill or find it particularly fascinating. In many training venues, sharing is encouraged, and discussions tend to flow freer about how this new knowledge can be applied. And sometime it's fun for the team just to play with new toys.

In one experience, a generally acknowledged dysfunctional team was permitted to stay together for the second phase of their project. At their members' insistence, they were all put through patterns training, platform-specific training, and specific tools training as a group. Consequently, in the very early days of the second phase of their project, it was apparent that they had gelled as a real team with a common vocabulary and a shared knowledge. The classroom situations allowed members to relax and to interact with one another as peers, because the material was new to practically everyone. The performance of the team in design activities was measurably improved, and morale recovered to the point that all members decided to remain together, despite the events of the previous phase. The break time from the project pressure cooker that was spent in the looser atmosphere of the classroom gave them the chance to see each other in a different light. "Gee," many of them thought, "these are human beings after all. Golly, I even *like* them!"

Training is only part of the answer, and this next suggestion usually gets managers shaking their heads. For newly formed teams without any experience in working together, a trial project may be required in which the team can apply its newly found knowledge. For example, units in an army, although trained in the same basic skills, still perform mock battle exercises to consolidate their team skills, as does any team. Software teams should be no different.

It's always desirable to consolidate expenditures and cut risks, and by team training you give everyone an equal opportunity to become valuable as well as to iron out potentially troublesome team issues. Sending the entire team through formal training sessions relevant to the project can do this.

> Therefore:
> Train the team as a unit in relevant technologies and soft skills if needed. Give everyone the same tools and language. The individual differences among members diminish as learning is shared. Additionally, team members become more familiar with one another's background, education, experience, and problem-solving approaches, as well as personal styles (see CULTURAL COMPETENCE(9)). Most important, the team is not using the project as the primary learning experience.

This pattern is most powerful when applied with TRIAL PROJECT (33)—find something to do with your new team training that has real value but isn't critical or large. When the real battle comes, the team is fit and ready to fight.

Cadet mounting plane prior to training flight. Craig Field, Southeastern Air Training Center, Selma, Alabama, 1941.

33

Trial Project

. . . if an army platoon is issued weapons and put together after advanced infantry training, are they now a fighting unit? If nine experienced baseball players are handed gloves, bats, and a ball, are they capable of playing as a team right away? If a group of four is handed the appropriate instruments, are they a string quartet? If a pilot has been through ground school and the simulator, is she ready to fly for a commercial air carrier? If an experienced software development team is run through training in relevant technology, are they immediately capable of employing it effectively as a team? Would you risk your company on it? Maybe you already have.

Training, exclusively, will not make a team effective. Application of knowledge in a real setting is essential, but risks must be kept to a minimum.

Photograph by John Collier, 1941; Library of Congress, Prints & Photographs Division, FSA-OWI Collection [LC-USF34-080370-D DLC].

After a team of experienced software developers is formed and put through training together (TRAIN HARD, FIGHT EASY(32)), they still are not totally prepared. Even though the training was in tools and technology, the new knowledge is truly useful only if it has been applied at least once. First mistakes are usually the largest and most costly, and it's far better to have them occur on less-critical tasks whenever possible. Of course, it's possible that having spent all this money on training, someone may be getting impatient to have some real work done. But as any veteran knows, the higher the stakes, the more preparation pays off.

Whether in sports, war, or the performing arts, the notion of training and practice is universal, yet in business, it seems we are so impatient to make some money that we try to vault over all these inconvenient and expensive preparation exercises. In some software development organizations, no matter how carefully people try to adhere to processes and to be very engineer-like in their development, with every project it seems as if they are starting completely over.

There can be several reasons for this. One, of course, is that each project is such a disaster that they really *have* to start over each time in order to wipe the emotional slate clean. Another reason may be that teams are constantly split up and the personnel redistributed and reformed into new teams. A third reason might be that the processes themselves are in a state of flux as paradigms shift or upper management issues an edict that the organization will reach SEI (Software Engineering Institute) Level 3 by the end of the year—*or else!* But let's assume that things are somewhat stable in the type of work you do and when you invest in tools it's for the long haul. Furthermore, if TRAIN HARD, FIGHT EASY(32) really was taken to heart, then you clearly have invested some time and money into a team you'd like to keep together for a while. Why not build a TRIAL PROJECT(33) together, using the new learned technology? Make it a real project, but a small one of no profound consequence. Call it "preseason."

Are your managers beginning to think that you train and practice as a way to dodge real responsibility? Will it ever pay off? It will. Beyond training, working through a small but real project helps the team learn to manage the dynamics of working together, using the new tools and methods recently learned with TRAIN HARD, FIGHT EASY(32). A brief project of some weight and consequence, but not show-stopping value, can really help to shake out the team's stiffness with the new lessons. It gives a team the opportunity to hit its stride, to learn to turn that double-play cleanly, to set up an ambush, or to implement clean code meeting the agreed-upon interfaces. Because success is more likely on a smaller effort, it gives the kind of reinforcement that makes a team feel battle-seasoned and ready to tackle something greater.

> Therefore:
> Find projects that are valuable but not terribly large or risky for a team's first foray together. Let them discover under real project conditions how, and how well, they work together under mild pressure. A brief project also provides some useful information about the team's strengths and weaknesses and what future risks will have to be mitigated when the larger projects commence.

This pattern is in some ways a variation of CASUAL DUTY(36), although it applies only to either newly formed teams or teams that have just been through training in new technologies together. CASUAL DUTY(36) applies more to teams you have an interest in keeping together between projects or as a means to integrate new members who are joining prior to a new development effort.

*Root cellar in Dead Ox Flat,
Malheur County, Oregon.*

34

Secret Stash

. . . Mrs. Wardlow has 500 quarts of food in her dugout cellar—just in case.

Pulling a rabbit out of a hat is fun. It amuses the audience most when the practice and preparation that went into the trick are not revealed. Naturally, if you haven't perfected the trick, then you don't perform it in public until you do, leaving none the wiser.

Some risks worth taking in pursuit of a significant technical or institutional advantage may be unacceptable to your superiors. In your judgment, to fail to advance the effort is an affront to the innovative spirit. You are determined to carry this out even if you are not officially supported because you believe the potential payoff to be attractive.

Photograph by Dorothea Lange, 1939; Library of Congress, Prints & Photographs Division, FSA-OWI Collection [LC-USF34-021469-E].

Sometimes one has an inkling of something that *just might work,* and its impact could be tremendous. A prototyping effort or some other form of exploration is essential. Unfortunately, there is a risk in taking such an effort public. It will either get quashed at the beginning as not worthy of official support or be trashed totally if it fails after being officially supported, killing future hopes for innovation. In such cases it might be better to quietly initiate the effort in an unofficial capacity by hiding it under some other name or existing project.

Creating a SECRET STASH(34) is the way a leader can protect innovative and strategic efforts. There are a number of ways it can be used, all of them a bit devious and all of them in the spirit of "'tis better to beg forgiveness than to ask permission." Often it may be nothing more than giving an ambitious engineer the go-ahead to try something she is certain can pay off. At other times, the effort is large enough to require the attention of a small team of developers, and this is when more adept bureaucratic tinkering is necessary. As in CONTAINMENT BUILDING(48) and CARGO CULT(49), the tinkering may be purely some sleight-of-hand with the organizational charts or names of things. Each instance of use of this pattern will need to be tailored to the specifics of its size, risk, potential payoff, and how visible it will be, no matter how well concealed, because some prototyping may require capital resources not easily disguised.

There is much that can go wrong in such a scheme. First, developers love to talk about their work, and the wrong audience could sink all of you, so it is essential that everyone understand the need for secrecy. Second, as tightly as some budgets and personnel are managed, it may be very dicey to dance around how everyone's time is being spent. You need to plan for every possible leak from and query into your secret activity. Third, such efforts can drain valuable resources from officially sanctioned efforts, so you'd better be sure that the payoff is worth it if that happens. And, finally, if the effort does fail, you must have an end game in place to deal with that failure. You must be prepared to FALL ON THE GRENADE(51).

However, there is much that can go right. Not only do you have the opportunity to support real innovation in your company, you also are keeping your team creatively engaged. In one telecommunications laboratory, the team was not only *allowed* but *expected* to vigorously seek new opportunities. At the beginning there was not always an accounting number to charge these activities to, so the manager bore the burden for the team by actively working with them on their time sheets to creatively balance out the numbers to make sure they passed by unchallenged. Never was a bean counter's alarm triggered, and no actuarial bells were jangled. The ultimate result of this covert activity was an inordinate number of patents generated by this very satisfied team, peer esteem for the manager, and downright jealousy when the strategic dollars were doled out annually. Over time it had become a matter of fiduciary responsibility that all the strategic dollars were to go to this manager.

Yes, it may be devious and possibly wrong to do such things, but keep in mind that one very large and successful company, Lockheed-Martin, institutionalized this practice by building a large part of their business on what they call a "Skunk Works." The people at Lockheed found out long ago that sometimes seeking permission is more costly than taking a stealthy chance.

Therefore:
Take the risk! Hide the effort inside another organizational box or under the guise of something slightly different but more politically palatable. Inform the people working on the unofficial prototype what cover story they must use if questioned. Finally, accept full responsibility if it is discovered, fails utterly, or threatens your developers with punishment. If it succeeds, praise the developers to the sky. If you do make magic, your bosses will love you, but they'll have to get in line behind your developers to show you how much.

Unemployed youth in Washington, DC.

35

Defeat

. . . high-tech culture, as well as society in general, tends to be very achievement oriented. High-performance gurus tell us that by making simple changes in our lives we will experience unbounded success like we've never felt or dreamed possible. Yet, despair and defeat are conditions that every person will know in life.

As a manager, you find yourself living in fear of defeat, fear of the consequences and repercussions that you will experience if your project goes up in flames. Your fear finds you treading carefully in all your decisions and taking the low-risk route whenever possible. Your fear is holding you back.

Photograph by John Vachon, 1938; Library of Congress, Prints & Photographs Division, FSA-OWI Collection [LC-USF34-008594-D DLC].

Too many books and training programs and popular contemporary myths capitalize on the notion of creating and establishing success. However, every manager and software developer with enough experience will know defeat. In fact, without such experience, any high-tech player is not yet fully prepared for the depth of her environs. Defeat is always possible when risks are taken, and if a leader has a career in which risks are not a factor, then it is likely that her career has not required much, rendering her a sleepy bureaucrat. In a world without risks, leaders are unnecessary. Without risks life becomes static.

The tension that quivers between victory and defeat is one of the prime sources of feeling alive, and feeling that one's life is meaningful. Unless you just came out of college into a lucrative job market, you are acutely aware that you accepted a new level of risk as you moved into the role of manager. You may not have recognized that at the time, but it has become clear over time. It keeps you awake at night. But consider an alternative thesis in your consideration of failure: Only by embarking upon quests in which defeat is a possibility can a leader have a measurable effect on events and delight in victory. The road to defeat is as instructional and informative as any path to another outcome. Defeat itself tests a manager in ways that are unique and cannot be simulated or imagined.

Projects will be late, budgets will be busted, people will clash or fail or sabotage, and you will sometimes grossly misjudge things and be left with blame and ruins. This is not terminal. Your career is elastic and adaptive. If you are truly good at what you do, if you are one who leads, rather than drives, people into the teeth of adversity, you should feel as accepting of defeat as of victory. Until you retire or die, there is no final play, nothing that in itself can wholly define you.

We hear of goal-oriented and results-based viewpoints, but perhaps these are too limited. These views try to make the continuous discrete; they atomize the stream. We don't believe it is enough to measure success by salary, by the number of people managed, or by the revenue brought in. Stop marking your career in terms of the highs and low, and measure, instead, the inflection points. Note the trends. Take account of your success by enjoying the relationships you have grown and the satisfaction that you see in the people around you. Scores are perfect for sports, but in our lives, a score can never capture the essence of happiness or sadness nor plot our location in the web of our relationships.

Leave it to others and their folly to gloat in little victories and agonize over petty defeats and trite wins. Think instead of the near and distant field of possibilities that stretches into your future. You can cover but a thin path across this field but its potential is limitless.

Therefore:
When faced with a risky situation, don't turn away out of a fear of failure. Maintain your perspective at a large scale. When defeat does greet you, embrace it as a teacher. Be humble. Fuel the next campaign with the knowledge.

Rehabilitation client cleaning barn. Itasca County, Minnesota, 1939.

36

Casual Duty

. . . a team between projects is like an abandoned house, just waiting to be picked over by opportunistic managers. What do you do with a team with nothing to do just now?

When a team is between projects, with uncertainty as to when the next assignment may arrive, there is a temptation to split the team up and send its members off to other projects. If this team has been successful, there is a value in keeping it together, and surely if the team members desire to stay together, it serves no one to split them up. Effective teams are hard enough to build, so splitting an effective one up really makes no sense. Trouble is, they're not generating any revenue right now; and if they're truly idle, they get bored.

Photograph by John Vachon, 1939. Library of Congress, Prints & Photographs Division, FSA-OWI Collection [LC-USF34-060205-D DLC].

A team that stays together, stays focused, improves the relationships among its members, and produces work that is useful to their core knowledge base is ready for the next challenge. It's a pretty good bet that there are dozens of things you wish there was time to do or to build in your organization. Some examples:

◆ Tools that could make life easier for developers

◆ Training on and integration of third-party products

◆ Prototypes and theories to try out

◆ Infrastructure and frameworks that you keep meaning to build

◆ Processes to document (see LEVIATHAN(3))

If you have a team coming off a project whose members want to stay together and there's a fair chance that some revenue-generating proposition will come in sooner or later, it makes sense to keep the members together. Focus them on a task that needs doing but that takes a back seat to profit-oriented development if and when it comes up. By offering your team's services to other managers, you might even earn some favors that you can call in later. Everyone has jobs he wishes he had the time to do. When your team supplies another with a cool test tool, for example, your team will be building bridges that benefit the team, you, and the organization.

In one organization, management was wise enough to keep one team together between projects. During this time the team designed and built an architectural framework that it had been casually discussing as something pretty neat to fool around with. Unfortunately, no one wanted to take the risk of trying to do this in the context of a schedule-challenged project. In just the few weeks that they were "idle," the team built the framework and got it working well enough to build confidence that it was indeed worthy of real-world use. The team's manager protected it from raiders and upper-management scrutiny by various means, some of them perhaps questionable, but her faith paid off handsomely. This framework went on to pay for itself with time savings *and* a successful deployment of several commercial products built upon it. Along with the framework, two developers, enthused to be free to play with ideas they'd had, produced a couple of tools for project management and load, aiding current and future product development. Finally, the exercise really helped the team members to unite technically, with a good definition of roles and working relationships. When the next revenue-generating opportunity came their way, they tore into it with a vengeance, applying their new tools effectively and efficiently. The framework they developed eventually won them their company's highest technical award.

The term *casual duty* comes from the military. While awaiting orders and clearances and otherwise between jobs, soldiers are assigned to casual teams, which are employed to take on the tasks that don't require full-time attention but are vital, nonetheless. Such teams are used very flexibly, and participation in them seems to build morale and occasionally new skills. It is true that sometimes CASUAL DUTY(36) consists of picking up cigarette butts on the parade ground or using a sling-blade to whack weeds in a vacant lot, but often it is meaningful work that benefits both the organization and the team. Even when it is menial labor, the camaraderie that develops from shared labor does a lot to build cohesion in the unit.

> Therefore:
> Assign the team some fundamental work on infrastructure, tools, process, or whatever will benefit it, or other teams, in the future, to protect team members from corporate raiders, and to keep their gears humming synchronously.

There is some caution to be observed in applying this pattern for too long. Developers who are sidelined for extended periods doing work that does not address their need for creative expression may begin contemplating defection. Furthermore, be up front about what you're doing with them and how long you anticipate it lasting.

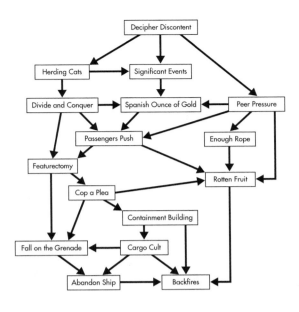

IV

Tactical Patterns

The patterns that we call tactical *are specific to situations you may encounter at various points in the development cycle or during the formation of a team. Some deal with stimulating positive action, others with minimizing negative occurrences, and still others with buying time or saving a team in distress, even when it is you who might be sacrificed in the short term. In short, finding the right action to take is what we are most interested in discovering. As one would expect of patterns, these can be applied and combined in an infinite number of ways and are most effective when used collectively rather than singly.*

37

Spanish Ounce of Gold

"Whosoever of ye raises me a white-headed whale with a wrinkled brow and a crooked jaw; whosoever of ye raises me that white-headed whale, with three holes punctured in his starboard fluke—look ye, whosoever of ye raises me that same white whale, he shall have this gold ounce, my boys!"

—Captain Ahab of the Pequod [1]

. . . salaries, promotions, general kudos, and the admiration of one's fellow developers become almost abstract ideas. Sometimes some reward above and beyond the normal expected returns can spur extraordinary efforts when they are needed most.

There may be very tough problems looming that can threaten the pace of development, the schedule, or even the entire development effort. This is when

1. Melville, Herman (1983). *Moby Dick.* New York: *Literary Classics of the United States, 965.*

you need extraordinary focus from each individual to find a solution, by any means necessary, as soon as possible.

Even the most exciting development efforts can become a little humdrum and the developers less caring about the long-term outcome. Issues that might be show-stoppers crop up, and no one seems concerned enough to alter priorities and to really, *really* dive into the issue and deal with it. There might be a rhythm to what everyone is already doing, and no one wants to threaten her own progress to take on a risky challenge.

As the boss, you could assign the troublesome item to someone or even use PEER PRESSURE(41) by assigning it to a pair of engineers. There are alternatives to this, however, that allow the individual engineers to make those decisions themselves. Putting a prize before them can stimulate the competitive urges among them that might have become dormant. It might also stimulate those who desire more explicit recognition of their genius. Or, if you have some cash-strapped or particularly money-grubbing team members, posting a prize of hard monetary value will get their juices flowing.

This may offend your notion of what it means to be professional, but it might be fun to entertain the baser impulses among us every now and then. If all the reasons software developers do what they do were distilled out, many of the lumps would be marked as money. Corporate awards of any substance always involve remunerative parts in thousands of dollars, or they aren't taken seriously. For your development staff to take grave problems seriously, you'll need to make any stakes high and up front, announcing exactly what they stand to gain should any rise to the challenge.

What's interesting is that in parts of the organization other than development, this is the primary method of motivation. Upper-level management and executive-level people are driven by explicit and lucrative rewards for high performance. Sales and marketing people are also given the incentive of potential riches for landing the big deals. This is especially true when revenue can immediately be recognized. Developers, sadly, are left out of this game for the most part. It seems patently unfair to us to provide nothing more than the possibility of a coffee cup, some movie tickets, or a dinner out when the expedient dispatch of a pesky problem could save thousands, tens of thousands, or even millions of dollars. Developers do respond to heartfelt thanks and to wide recognition in front of their peers, but you can't hold this out as a credible award to entice them into the breach of risk. By announcing a specific and lucrative reward for a specific accomplishment, you show that you recognize both the risks and the payoff for the effort requested, and that you are willing to pass on a piece of that payoff to whoever should solve the riddle. It's irresistible.

There is the danger, of course, that *everyone* will jump to the call and other valuable work will be neglected or that a refined sense of teamwork will slip, so the use of the SPANISH OUNCE OF GOLD(37) must be careful and rare. Ahab, to his credit, established very clearly to his crew where his priorities lay. They couldn't shirk their regular duties day to day, but he gave them the incentive they needed to do that extra bit to get Ahab what he most wanted.

> Now this doubloon was of the purest, virgin, gold, raked somewhere out of the heart of gorgeous hills, whence, east and west, over golden sands, the headwaters of Pactolus flows. And though now nailed amidst all the rustiness of iron bolts and the verdigris of copper spikes, yet, untouchable and immaculate to any foulness, it still preserved its Quito glow.[2]

The reward you post must shine through the "rustiness of iron bolts and the verdigris of copper spikes" of your development environment to be ever in the minds of the developers, to be felt by them like an insatiable itch that must needs be scratched.

Therefore:
Post an extraordinary reward, something of real value—like Ahab's 16-dollar gold piece nailed to the mast—to be claimed by the person or team that solves the knotty problem. Make the criteria clear so that no ambiguity exists about the solution, which must be testable or provable beyond a doubt. And what we're talking here is real, hard money—cash, moolah, bread, dough, scratch—whatever you want to call it—or its obvious equivalent, such as a boat, a lease on a car, or whatever would really get your developers' attention.

---

2. Ibid., 1253.

How the authors met.

38

Significant Events

. . . . processes drive software projects, even chaotic ones, and even when there are discrete points in a process, they are usually bland milestones or pointless measurements of completion of one thing or another. Geometric shapes on charts represent significant process events, but by themselves represent nothing that moves the human soul.

People need memorable events to mark the passage of the time of their lives and to remember the exercise of their labor as resulting in meaningful accomplishment.

As the schedule is reviewed in a Gantt chart projected in an overhead, the faces of the developers open in yawns as the project manager notes that version 1.16, revision E, of the requirements document has been approved by all concerned parties.

In celebration, he waves a laser pointer over the little black diamond. Even the completion of a hard-fought development effort ends in nothing more than a transfer of files to a release control organization and some last-minute reviews of release notes. This is not the sort of thing that inspires anthems to be written or chests to swell with pride.

Some software people are fortunate enough to work in industries that do have dramatic milestones. The pyrotechnics of a space shuttle launch provide many developers with an exciting event to mark the progress of their labors. Some engineers in the telephone switching business have participated in dramatic ceremonies of physically cutting cables during central office switch changeovers. A new fly-by-wire aircraft making its maiden voyage might provide such a thrill, particularly when filled with corporate executives. However, for the vast majority of software developers working on information systems, or in the telecom business, or in manufacturing, nothing much earthshaking really happens. That's a terrible shame.

The mythology of human endeavor is the expression of significant events. Time and progress were indelibly marked. We have encoded in our hearts and minds a need and a desire to have signposts on which to hang our memories and with which to anchor ourselves in time and place. Think of the first lunar landing, or of the flight of the *Spirit of St. Louis* over the Atlantic, or of Nelson Mandela walking free after 20 years of imprisonment. Around these armatures revolve entire global memories. In our personal lives, it is a marriage, a birth, a graduation, or perhaps an athletic victory by which we measure the large chunks of time as we pass our lives. SIGNIFICANT EVENTS(38) stand like tall signposts by which we orient ourselves.

In 1065, the year before William the Conqueror became the last invader of the British Isles, Sunset Crater in Arizona (USA) blew its volcanic heart out in a great explosion of lava, rain of fire, and hurtling bombs. Ancestors of today's remaining pueblo tribes, having wisely evacuated, must have seen quite a show. From that time on, everything was measured as having happened before, during, or after the blast.

Consider such grandeur in contrast with the day-to-day events that pass as markers to the cube-dwellers of the software world. Does it seem so odd that for many such people time has no measure and that the seasons and years are indistinguishable from one another? Deprived of the reminders of the physical world and within the safe environs that modern life provides, a blanket of blandness covers the days. Nothing bad really happens, but nothing memorable—nothing memorable in a visceral sense—ever really happens either. We work, we collect our pay, we take our measly two-week vacations, and then one day we arrive at retirement and wonder what we did with the time of our lives that we devoted to our work. *The End of Time* by polymath, pundit, poet, and proletarian Cardon Stimson contains this scene:

JACK: I had a job once. I suppose it was a good job. The days were very long. People said it was a good job. But the days were very long.

JANE: Yes?

JACK: Yes, and they were endless—yes, just endless, one after another.

JANE: Yes?

JACK: Yes. But that wasn't the worst thing.

JANE: No?

JACK: No. The worst thing was that it was very boring. It never changed. Nothing really happened.

JANE: Never?

JACK: No, never, and it went on for 27 years.

JANE: And then?

JACK: And then I woke up. Just like that. I asked myself a question.

JANE: What was the question?

JACK: I asked myself, "Why am I living the way I'm living?"

JANE: And?

JACK: And I answered, "For the money."

JANE: Only money?

JACK: Yes, and, well, for what the money could buy.

Nothing really happened. We get our one-year anniversary at the company, maybe our fifth, or twentieth, with the attendant company gifts accompanied by a smattering of applause, although most come for the free cake. We earn the extra perks that time served provides. We measure our time this way until we get to our mid-40s when the countdown toward retirement begins. Projects come and go, gradually blending into one another. We struggle to remember which year a particular product was first released, if we even care to remember at all. Wouldn't it be lovely if every now and then we had a truly significant event to celebrate, to bind our timelines to?

> Therefore:
> Devise, contrive, invent, or create *something* that will mark the milestones of your projects in a way that will really mean something to your team. Wrestle an alligator or box a kangaroo. Take the team to see something spectacular, or do something wild like a team parachute out of a plane. Shake it up!

Cat and her kittens, Canyon County, Idaho.

39

Herding Cats

"Nothing is more difficult, and therefore more precious, than to be able to decide."

—Napoleon I

. . . consensus building can increase loyalty and commitment among team members by involving everyone in the decision-making processes. Yet software systems are highly detailed and obscure, leaving little room for comprehensive discussion (see LEVIATHAN(3)).

You know the importance of having buy-in from *all* the team participants in order to increase productivity and creativity. You believe that empowered developers will work harder for the team and company, making your job that

---

Photograph by Russell Lee, 1941; Library of Congress, Prints & Photographs Division, FSA-OWI Collection [LC-USF34-039735-D DLC].

much easier. You are trying to reach consensus with your team, but you can't reach agreement on even the most capricious of ideas.

Your team discussions keep getting derailed by ethereal conversations about broad issues and goals or dreadful details that are draining and boring. Even though you're a technology team whose decisions should be bounded by rational thinking, you find yourself using the phrase, "my sense is . . ." repeatedly. In every attempt to convey the big picture, you find yourself surrounded by glazed-over eyes perched on slumped bodies, with one or two hyper developers who seem to pounce on your every word. You know it is incumbent on the leader to motivate and move everyone in the same direction, but this is ridiculous.

Consensus building, when used as a management device, is a lot like herding cats and will probably not produce the results you are striving for. In fact, you may find that you have spawned dissension among the team members when it becomes impossible to reach agreement on the issues. While *consensus building* may seem like the right thing to do to get a team motivated and aligned, for many managers it is just a way of expressing a proclivity for micromanagement.

It is much more productive to have your whole team agree on what the high-level, succinctly stated goals are for the project. It is not necessary to agree on every detail:

Develop a peer-to-peer software system to share digital music files on the Internet.

versus:

Architect and implement a peer-to-peer digital communication system that is founded upon a series of lightweight, asynchronous threading routines written in C++. It is crucial to apply the LinkZinc foundational libraries upon the IP multicast stack provided by Redballs Computing.

Now you've started a war. For the practitioners of multifarious fundamental religions, there can be no consensus. Avoid religious wars.

It is your job to assign the tasks and to manage accountability within your team, as well as to work with the appropriate experts on your team to fill out the details. Trust your experts to help you in this area. But *you* are the leader. Don't expect your developers to pick up the slack for you by hashing out every little detail in some interminable meeting—be a SHAMELESS IGNORAMUS(14). When your developers do speak, don't derail them or insult them by asking the system administrator if she agrees with the senior architect.

In one dot com startup we are familiar with, more than a million dollars went swirling down the toilet in a matter of weeks (and much more now that the company has declared bankruptcy), simply because the leadership could not make a decision and stick with it. It wasn't a lack of great ideas, just a lack of ability to focus on the right issues, such as hiring the experts they needed and then trusting the team members to handle their jobs. For even the most technical decisions, such as choosing server software or writing functional specifications, the business development personnel, the programmers, and the marketing team were brought in for a discussion of the pros and cons. The thrashing was scintillating and spectacular. On one occasion, the technical experts became so frustrated with how they were being overlooked in technical discussions that they plotted with one of the business leads ahead of time to have him agree with all of their opinions. Consensus was finally reached by virtue of blatant manipulation.

Your employees might think you are too vague and are attempting to keep all the power by controlling the information. More likely, they won't even notice, because they can go back to their miserable cubes and work on their designs and software. If they get to participate in defining the high-level goals with the parameters your company leadership or client has defined for the project, they will probably feel satisfied and have a positive stake in the outcome. Having clear goals is also a great way to hold your developers accountable. Delegating the technical specifics of implementation to the developers is always wiser than inviting review from those external to the development team.

> Therefore:
> Defy the temptation to reach a state of agreement on every detail. Instead, inspire a goal-oriented technology team by discussing and agreeing on the higher-level goals that invite enthusiasm, clarity, and ownership of the outcome of the project, but which leave plenty of room for the creative self-expression that will intrinsically reward dedicated developers.

ONE BY ONE(31), GEEK CHANNELING(12), DIVIDE AND CONQUER(40), and GET A GURU(21) all complement this pattern in various contexts.

US government photo from the Bureau of Land Reclamation.

40

Divide and Conquer

. . . the only way to eat a big piece of watermelon is in bites, not by shoving the whole thing in your mouth. You might choke. Of course, to really enjoy eating watermelon, you have to get your ears wet.

Making decisions on your team is like pulling teeth without anesthesia. Decisions are never made in an expedient manner, and the project schedule and team's enthusiasm suffer. You want everyone's buy-in to move forward, but team-based decision making is just not fast or effective.

You have managed to put together a team of smart, diverse, and opinionated powerhouses. Your incredibly bright developers are very impressive when they start discussing their particular niches (even though you tend to be about a step behind everything they say). You try not to interfere, knowing that you are the SHAMELESS

Photo found at http://www.usbr.gov/history/mellon.jpg.

171

IGNORAMUS(14). You've been exercising GEEK CHANNELING(12), much to your great amusement, but there are still times when it is imperative that you bring your group together to solve a project problem.

Typically, the sticking point has more to do with the size of the group trying to solve the problem than with either the people or the problem itself. With the number of communication links rising exponentially with the number of people involved, especially if the people are engineers who look at every aspect before rendering a decision, you have a combinatorial explosion every time you need a swift decision. Split them up, try a variation of PEER PRESSURE(41) if you have to, but shrink the group to fit the task. You'll have shorter team meetings, get more done, and have grateful team members who don't have to make up excuses about why they can't come to the meeting this week. In smaller working groups, people have a better chance of being heard, and even have their ideas tossed out with less emotional risk.

This also works well for cross-fertilizing expert opinions across projects or areas of aptitude, although this is contrary to many conventional models of team structure. Consider the fairly common form, the SWAT Team, described by Steve McConnell:

> In software, "SWAT" stands for "SKILLED WITH ADVANCED TOOLS." . . . The idea behind a SWAT team is to take a group of people who are highly skilled with a particular tool or practice and turn them loose on a problem that is well suited to being solved by that tool or practice.[1]

While the authors can see great value in this SWAT approach, as we describe similarly in PEER PRESSURE(41), we feel that creativity is risked when one segregates personnel by skill set. Oddly enough, in McConnell's description of a SWAT team, he notes that each member of a traditional military SWAT team is highly trained in a *different* specialty, such as explosives or high-speed driving, for maximum capability in a crisis. He further notes, "Their job is not to be creative but to implement a solution within the limits of a tool or a practice. . . ."[2] Contrarily, we believe that this artificially limits human creativity—even if they are great JINI programmers—and should be avoided at all costs. This approach will blow up in your face, even if it seems to solve a few problems in the short run. Not only will team members become bitter, but they will also become less valuable to you as their skills weaken in other disciplines.

---

1. McConnell, Steve (1996). *Rapid Development*. Redmond, WA: Microsoft Press, 308.
2. Ibid., 309.

A good example of this pattern involved a manager who divided her team into smaller groups for weekly meetings. This particular team included a software geek, an anthropologist, and the manager herself who was a computer-human interaction expert. She produced a loose agenda that seemed constrained only by the limits of "tell me what's going on." The advantages to this approach seemed enormous—sometimes it was a forum to complain and whine about the company, at other times a haywire employee's behavior would percolate to the surface, and at other times grandiose discussions of war and peace became pertinent. Mistakes were avoided by having the opportunity to verbalize solutions and their potential impacts early, other solutions were justified, and seemingly inane conversations led to novel ideas that morphed into patents or into clients who begged to know what "the process" was for coming up with such unique propositions.

This manager broke through the competitive tendencies we often find among software developers and helped form lasting bonds among peers. In fact, this particular manager got nailed on occasion for her lack of effective GEEK CHANNELING(12) and for failing to follow the established processes, but her ability to effectively exercise this pattern ultimately saved her position when chaos inevitably settled like a swarm over the organization.

> Therefore:
> Use small teams of experts to your advantage when solving a problem. Don't have your whole team waste time discussing a technical detail that two people can solve. Use small breakout teams that are organized in some logical fashion and that can return to the team with a solution that all can trust and use. You may have to appoint the members of your breakout teams, but solicit the input of your developers. They know who's got the skinny on your problem. You can further your knowledge about the problem in a more controlled setting where you aren't boring the masses, and your developers can spend time with you puzzling over your problem and strutting their stuff.

This pattern should be and can be mixed with various uses of PASSENGERS PUSH(42), ONE BY ONE(31), PEER PRESSURE(41), and HERDING CATS(39). Your particular uses will vary according to context, personnel, and the alignment of the planets.

East German Grepos "protecting" workmen.

41

Peer Pressure

. . . despite the most controlling, detail-oriented management imaginable, there are always loose ends, sudden discoveries, or mistaken assumptions that spawn additional responsibilities for the team. Although these duties may be external to the main thrust of the project, they are still vital to the life of the project.

Engineers, once focused on their mission, treat peripheral duties too lightly or believe that nothing can supplant their primary responsibilities. Yet peripheral duties always seem to intrude. You want to keep their momentum going, and priorities might get muddled if you start assigning additional duties. Besides, developers set their own priorities unless some mechanism can be established that ensures that all assigned tasks will be accomplished.

Frequently in a project, no matter what the state of its completion, strange things happen. Under pressures of schedule, fluid requirements, mutating technology, and the whims of corporate leadership, getting "redirected" should never be surprising to either you or the team. These things must be resolved thoroughly and efficiently—and soon. A project may be under tight schedule pressures, but pesky, nontrivial side issues keep coming up, some of which may be critical to the project. You hate to distract engineers with these things, but they must be resolved somehow.

Two people equally responsible for something are more likely to do a good job of producing the result than a single person acting alone. This occurs for two reasons: First, the dialog between the people balances their individual prejudices, and second, each ensures that the other doesn't slack off. Or rather, neither will be derelict in his duties because he wants to maintain his respect and reputation with his peer. In pairing people who actually hold opposite views, you may reap the benefits of putting thesis and antithesis in close quarters; you may reap a creative *synthesis* in the solution. Additionally, a side effect of pairing one developer with another who is critical of the former's ideas or approach is the delegation of the working out of their differences to them. These emergent phenomena can be well worth the risk of using this approach.

Although the motivation for such pairing may have its roots in an unsavory historical phenomenon, the actual affect of these pairings plays on what is a very positive and self-motivated sense that good engineers possess—image in the eyes of their peers.

When the Berlin Wall still stood, the East German army always assigned guards in pairs to border posts. The guards were always from different areas of the country and were never familiar to one another.

> They have been forced to operate in pairs and are never permitted to know their partner beforehand.[1]

Additionally, each was totally responsible for the behavior of the other—if one of them defected across the border, the other would be punished for not using even lethal means to stop him.

> . . . If they miss an escapee at the frontier, they are sent to prison for complicity in that escape.[2]

---

1. Nelson, Walter Henry (1969). *The Berliners.* New York: David McKay Company, 190.
2. Ibid., 198.

Though sinister, it worked very well to ensure that the mission was accomplished.[3] In the project context, it is meant to be less punitive but equally effective in helping to ensure that both parties hold up their end of the responsibility. The fact that it is fear of disapproval or loss of face, rather than a heavy rain of 7.62-mm rounds, does not diminish its effectiveness. Egos aside, the opinions of one's peer group carry more weight than do the opinions of management. Always have, always will.

The frightening example of East German *Grenzpolizei,* or "Grepos," is not reassuring and may not be entirely convincing. But there is a positive side effect in pairing developers not well known to each other: It further strengthens the web of relationships that makes up the team. This is a way to help break down the walls of any cliques that may exist in the team, particularly a newly formed team. Often, when new teams are formed from fragments of other teams, there are small groups of developers who have formed strong personal relationships in the earlier effort and carry this to the new team. Sometimes this can create an "insider/outsider" effect, and those individuals who are not as assertive or outgoing will be marginalized. Pairing one of these people with an individual already comfortable and connected in the new team can go a long way toward integrating them all together. In fact, even in our Grepo example, this tendency brought even wary partners along the border to create bonds that superseded the training and fear that had been instilled in them against such relationships.

> It wasn't enough for one guard to watch his companion on duty; now a
> third was assigned to watch them both.[4]

This scenario is unlikely in the software development world, so relax. We're not trying to cast you into the role of evil commissar. The positive outcome of such pairings will reward the judicious use of this pattern in both improving the interaction of the team and uncovering creative solutions to unexpected problems.

Therefore:
Always assign a pair of engineers to be responsible for resolving peripheral project issues. It is most effective if the pair does not always see eye-to-eye on

---

3. In truth, the hardening of the frontier barriers was also essential to diminishing the numbers of guards who defected to the West, although no amount of hardening could have stopped guards who had no fear of their partners.
4. Nelson, *supra,* 196.

things all the time. In fact, it is optimal if they don't even know each other well and have never collaborated before. They are equally responsible for a positive outcome to the assignment.

This is a more severe variant of PASSENGERS PUSH(42), but it comes highly recommended based on the experience of the authors and others.

Pushing the truck of a migrant family en route to California in order to get it started, near Henrietta, Oklahoma, 1939.

42

Passengers Push

. . . sometimes you have to all jump out and help to get the car started before anyone can ride to California, and even when you get to the Golden State, it doesn't end there.

In San Francisco, California, millions of people ride the cable car system that moves throughout the city. Operated by a gripman on the brakes, the cable cars are powered by loops of steel cable that move continuously under the street. San Francisco is very hilly, and when the cars are loaded down, they have trouble cresting the largest hills, so several passengers will jump out spontaneously and push the cable car over the top.

At critical moments during a project, one or two developers can get bogged down with the most difficult work. Because of the interrelationships of the code

Photograph by Lee Russell, 1939; Library of Congress, Prints & Photographs Division, FSA-OWI Collection, [LC-USF33-012322-M4].

itself and the partitions created between ownership of various parts of the system, the majority of the development will halt until certain critical items are completed.

One or two hang-ups like this can slip a project severely and permanently throw off the development schedule. Cycles are lost, and it's unwise to send waiting developers off on a parallel track that may engulf them, derail them, and cause the whole problem to occur again. This is often the direct result of project managers and other similarly fixated folk, who insist on applying the concept of *ownership* to discrete, and often arbitrary, elements of the entire project. Although there may be an effort to affix the proper deliverable to the most appropriate programmer, the end result is that the programmer and the deliverable are never separated except by death or some other kind of separation event. Not only does that schedule get repeatedly threatened by the bottlenecks created by the *one developer-one problem* paradigm, the end result may never be as good as it could have been.

It is often the nature of the geek to thrash about a problem when it becomes difficult, as if brute force, more coffee, and some time to concentrate will ultimately carry him through. It is true that the developer will deliver something that appears to perform as desired, yet the quality may be questionable. Asking for help from other programmers feels shameful and can sometimes lead to lousy advice anyway because the go-to guy has no clue either. If the developer is lucky, there is a guru on staff with whom he can speak about his problem, show her the code, and hope that he hasn't done something incredibly daft and humiliating. Of course, if the developer with the problem is the guru herself, then this is not so simple. Software coding problems become more ego-bound as they reveal their complexity. All that may be needed is a pair of fresh eyes or some alternative insights.

It is not hard for a developer to get caught in a web of conceit only to be exacerbated by the sadists who created the favored project management software. All the features designed to clarify the constants and variables simply add to the confusing morass and ultimately heighten the tension when the carefully delineated artifacts slip out of position. Woe to you who think it is your job to walk around with a pen marking in the *percent complete* box. If you've survived one software project, you know that it is impossible to anticipate the scope of a particular deliverable, how long it will take, and the percent of effort it will require before a developer has even begun to understand just what it is that she has been asked to design, create, and deliver.

It's all too common to make a ludicrous covenant like this for each project kick-off and then be forced to live with it.

There is a hot new development methodology called *eXtreme Programming* that recommends ways to manage projects that have rapidly changing requirements with rapid development cycles. These theorists have defined a rule in their methodology that they call *Collective Ownership*—that any developer can change any line of code. The process is managed by designing a unit test as the primary task when a developer is creating new code. This automates the testing of every change that is implemented: "Once this is in place, anyone can make a change to any method of any class and release it to the code repository as needed. When combined with *frequent integration,* developers rarely even notice a class has been extended or repaired."[1]

This is just methodology, but it is very revealing. We're astounded by the conditions of software engineering that create an environment in which it is revolutionary to suggest that members of the same team trust each other. Furthermore, we believe that by creating a coerced adherence to a Gantt chart, which at best is largely ignored and at worst alienates the programmers from each other, you introduce a foolish sense of competitiveness. After all, rushing to deliver a piece of software to be reflected well on the schedule is misguided.

Like the passengers who spontaneously jump off the cable car in order to push it over the top, your developers should feel motivated to help push the entire project forward, not just their discrete, enumerated efforts. Your developers should know that if they aren't willing to get out and push that they will never arrive at their destination—neither on time nor together.

How can you keep track of what's going on? How are you expected to hold your programmers to a simple deadline if you haven't garnered their commitment up front? You can do it by establishing a sense of collective ownership for the results—make it clear that we are in this together. If one goes down, we all go down. Facilitate this by providing frequent opportunities for meaningful communication—short meetings or breakout teams as described in DIVIDE AND CONQUER(40). Don't be tempted to have long, drawn-out project meetings to flog every detail to the ground; in fact, without a traditional project plan you won't be able to do that. The tasks are still important, but we own all the tasks together.

---

1. http://www.extremeprogramming.org/rules/collective.html.

Therefore:
Establish a sense of collective ownership for *all* the elements of the project. The developers will feel sanctioned and compelled to put forth their best efforts on behalf of the team and their goal. Make it clear that their territory is the *whole* territory over which each and all may range and improve things as needed. The key to this is to provide frequent opportunities for communication between team members.

Extreme Programmers talk about pairing up programmers for maximum efficiency, and this rule should not be confused with the pattern, PEER PRESSURE(41). The patterns presented and discussed in SOCIAL JESTER(18) and HOME FIELD ADVANTAGE(22) should help you to determine how to create collective teams. Furthermore, there is always the danger of collective ownership degenerating into a chaotic mess if any developer starts getting change-crazy and doesn't coordinate with the other members. In such circumstances, it might be wise to use PEER PRESSURE(41).

Picket line at the King Farm strike, near Morrisville, Pennsylvania, 1938.

43

Decipher Discontent

. . . people in today's society are stressed. One day it's their family, the next it's their jobs, finally it's their hair. Stress releases hormones in the body, including adrenaline and cortisol, which, under prolonged conditions of expression, wear down the body. Ultimately, heart disease, impaired memory, and a depressed immune system set in. Yet, reducing stress requires a fundamental shift in attitude, which can be very difficult to create when the conditions of life contain multiple stress triggers.

You sense that there are real problems lurking that require your attention, but don't understand what the issues are that require immediate action.

Photograph by John Vachon, 1938; Library of Congress, Prints & Photographs Division, FSA-OWI Collection [LC-USF34-008587-D DLC].

Members of your development team grouse often about the company, the clients, and the overall neglect and discontent they feel in their day-to-day existence. Sometimes they seem overtly angry, sometimes times sarcastic, and often disdainful of you. Yet their feelings are difficult to pin down.

We observed in GREASE THE WHEEL(30) the need to listen closely to the complaints of a disruptive individual in the hope of either letting her simply air out or redirecting her to a more positive end. DECIPHER DISCONTENT(43), on the other hand, is more concerned with the dynamics of *group-wide* discontent—when the team is harmonious in its complaints. The team doesn't even try to make you squirm anymore—that sport has lost its thrill. This is serious angst that you are detecting. It is obvious that there are elements of the workplace experience that are driving this—after all, *all* the team members couldn't have bad marriages, a long commute, and kids in lock-up. When your entire team seems angry, something fundamental has gone awry, and you didn't notice soon enough to stave it off.

It is your responsibility to set the tone, whether it is by attitude, enthusiasm, humor, or with a healthy dose of sarcasm. Chances are, you have seriously failed your team if things have gotten so bad—either they are simply reflecting your sour attitude toward the company and the clients, or you have been so consumed with your own political machinations that you aren't leading anymore.

In one large company, the effects of a corporate strike ultimately decimated a high-performance team at its major research laboratory. One factor in the demise of the storied team was the inability of the manager who, after bailing his team out of the doldrums of their bizarre and often inhumane strike assignments, was never able to pull his own head out of the shadow of anger toward the company. At first it was just the individual complaints that got to him, then the mental breakdown of a colleague, and, finally, the insulting pittance offered to the employees who had stuck it out for the greater good of the corporation. He felt that the company had fundamentally changed his team. He couldn't see that he was feeding the team's discontent because he was so enraged by his own experiences. His depression was a constant reminder of all that had occurred. He was impotent to lead his team out of the morass. It was obvious that their leader had been battle scarred beyond recognition—his door shut all day, long lunches, golf during work hours, and total lack of interest in any of their efforts. While his discontent was borne of empathy for his team's experiences, the team was essentially left without a leader on the field of battle, and many of the team members simply retreated or moved on.

When your entire team seems to be disintegrating before your very eyes, getting to the source of the problem is the fundamental task at hand. Many of the symptoms won't directly indicate the problem—talk stops when you walk up, deadlines slip, and meeting attendance dries up. You will actually have to confront your team head on—over beers, lunch, or someplace neutral to the workplace. This is no time to be defensive or to provide pat little management kernels in hopes that you can put a bandage on the problem. Now is the time to really listen *without* judgment and to avoid the temptation to fix it all immediately. Besides, they may be upset with things so far out of your realm of control that you completely empathize with their distress, but can't do a damn thing to change it. Of course, it may be just you, and you need to be big enough to accept that truth if that's the reality of the situation. You will never know how to solve the problem until you know what it is. Ask.

No matter what the issue, it can't be solved unless someone is willing to stand up and lead the team forward. Your team is relying on your creative abilities as a leader to tease out the fundamental issues and to discover a way to move beyond them, for better or for worse. Your team will respect your attempts to clear the air, but be forewarned—do not violate the team's confidence by asking the members for the truth and then using it against them. That was one of the more charming characteristics of a friend we'll call Earl Fudge, who managed to gull his team into a frank and honest discussion of his shortcomings as a leader, and then gave each of those who had the temerity to criticize him very poor evaluations. This episode had a happy ending though, as several of the developers banded together and got Ol' Earl bounced. Take our word for it and avoid such practice.

If you ask for honesty, then be fair enough to accept it without acrimony or thoughts of revenge. If you can be trusted, now is the time to prove it.

Therefore:
Summon the courage and confront your team with the sole intention of airing out its members' concerns. Find out whether you have screwed up or whether there is a larger problem that you can take steps to resolve. Apologize for not addressing the issues sooner, and take responsibility for doing whatever it takes to work with the team to accept, confront, or duck whatever the looming issue is.

Discontent deciphered.

*A fire-blasted Ponderosa Pine
(left) and the fire lookout
tower on Mt. Elden, Arizona.*

44

Backfires

*. . . backfires are a technique used to control forest fires. A backfire is set in
the path of the main fire to remove fuel. Without fuel, a fire will not burn.
A backfire is not a guarantee of success in the control of a fire; a change in
wind direction or speed can transform a controlled backfire into a violent
conflagration.*

At the start of, and in the early phases of every project, experienced managers can identify risk factors that carry the possibility of flare-ups that can
immolate a project. Ignoring those factors is most certain to burn you in the
future. Mitigation also carries its own inherent risks.

Every project has difficulties that are painful to moderate, such as bug-ridden
tools, a problem person on the development team, lack of funding, or poor support

from corporate leadership. Even the talents of the manager become a risk factor, as shortcomings or errors in early planning and estimation are invariably revealed. The real trick to your effectiveness at this stage is to perceive which problems can be smoothed over quietly and which problems will rear up to bring it all down.

Much like attempting to block a fire in the diverse conditions of the wilderness, the timing and technique you employ to protect your project from future damage are based on your ability to understand the nature of the hazards. You do not deal with a cash flow problem in the same way that you deal with an employee who is having family problems, but both are obvious detrimental factors to a successful project outcome. It may be best to expose financial problems with a significant and very vocal emphasis on how funding is mapped to product outcome, but the troubled team member needs to be supported quietly and with compassion. Given the variety of vulnerabilities that are unique to each project, it is simply not possible to rely on one prescribed method. No strategy is risk-free. Doing nothing is absurd.

Your controls may fail and your preventive fire could jump the line, or, like a backfire in a roaring wind, your strategy may bring harm to your image as a strong leader. You may look weak or whiny and unwilling or unable to deal with adversity. Your more vicious colleagues will love it, and your supporters may turn their eyes in shame. Yet, we believe this is a small price to pay for the long-term gain you will reap—survival. It's best to do early whatever destruction you need to do. By tightening up your project parameters, budgets, and team members from the onset, you greatly increase the likelihood of ultimate success.

Acting early and with urgency may prevent you from a later FALL ON THE GRENADE(51) or a drowning project as in ABANDON SHIP(52). If you have an arrogant, troublesome person on the team, get him out now. If you need more money than you initially accounted for, expose your mistake and get what you need for the project. If your team is overcommitted, better to declare it early than to just hope for the best. By raising the issues now, you deny fuel for later criticism when it can really be damaging to more than just your ego. Small sacrifices earlier rather than later can surround you with a fuel-free zone so that if the project stalls or even fails you can watch the blaze of retribution roar around you but not burn you or your team members, because you have been proactive in seeking solutions.

Therefore:
Identify the risk factors in your project that carry the greatest probability of becoming damaging reality. Appropriately address these issues immediately with a sense of urgency and conviction. It may be enough to draw attention to

a problem, or drastic measures may be in order. Either way, the problem should be thoroughly and convincingly mitigated.

Dealing with specific problems is addressed extensively in ROTTEN FRUIT(46), HERDING CATS(39), FEATURECTOMY(47), INOCULATION (28), and PUSH THE CUSTOMER(26). These are techniques to build BACKFIRES(44).

Dudes learning how to throw a rope, "roping," during a ranch rodeo contest. Brewster Arnold Quarter Circle U Ranch, Birney, Montana.

45

Enough Rope

. . . you may be trying to GREASE THE WHEEL(30), but the wheel just won't stop squeaking. It may be time to help this one become self-lubricating.

Someone on your team just isn't making progress—always because of something needed, missing, or unavailable. Decrying lack of resources at each encounter, you suspect that he simply isn't putting in the effort.

Sometimes resources are the problem, and without the right tools, or expertise, or training, the job won't get done. Other times, however, it's the *will* to get things done that's missing, and the decrying of resource shortages is a smokescreen. You don't want to get into a debate about what developers really need to do their

Photograph by Marion Post Walcott, 1941; Library of Congress, Prints & Photographs Division, FSA-OWI Collection [LC-USF33-031288-M1 DLC].

jobs. Even if you prove you're right and win the battle, if the war goes awry, your tactical victory will come back to haunt you as your superiors ask why you didn't supply the necessary technology, consultant, and so on. Don't be TOO CLEVER BY HALF(15). If you suspect that someone is balking, and he claims it's for lack of something, then expect the best, give him the HOME FIELD ADVANTAGE(22), and get him what he asks for.

If you are lucky, the squeaky wheel will start rolling silently along, making real progress. At worst, it will be clearly revealed that it isn't a resource problem, and even if it was, well then, you solved it. Whatever the outcome, you will have enough information to take the next step to remove further obstacles.

Therefore:
Give the person everything he says is needed and more. Dedicate all the resources you can to supporting him so that all that remains is his effort to get the desired result. Eliminate all shelters from failure, all excuses.

Smoke him out, if necessary, and expose where the real problem lies. Whether the target individual sees what you're doing, or really does now have the tools to do the job doesn't matter. If you're lucky, the problem will repair itself. If not, it may be time to drop the ROTTEN FRUIT(46).

Fruits and vegetables, market square, Waco, Texas.

46

Rotten Fruit

You have a chronic troublemaker who is upsetting all your efforts by crossing you at every turn, dragging his feet, and being generally unpleasant in public forums.

This complainer is starting to spoil the whole team by his disruptions and is distracting from the overall focus. You've applied PEER PRESSURE(41) and tried to GREASE THE WHEEL(30). You may have handed him ENOUGH ROPE(45), but he still complains. He is sapping your resources and costing you the efforts of a valuable productive programmer. This malcontent is often a hotshot developer, and it is hard to imagine giving up resources at this point in the process.

Photograph by Lee Russell, 1939; Library of Congress, Prints & Photographs Division, FSA-OWI Collection [LC-USF33-012515-M5 DLC].

Dealing effectively and immediately with problem personnel demonstrates to your team that you are on their side, are personally aware of their needs, and will act accordingly. By understanding the pattern THE GAUNTLET(25), you are aware that your team is actually exposing the annoying team member to you. Take the hint, and you will continue to engender trust with your productive and contributing team members.

McConnell notes the extensive data that shows how management oversight can unalterably damage the morale of your team by not handling the obstinate, stubborn, mule-headed hack:

> In a review of 32 management teams, Larson and LaFast found that the most consistent and intense complaint from team members was that their team leaders were unwilling to confront and resolve problems associated with poor performance by individual team members (Larson and LaFast 1989). They report that "[m]ore than any other single aspect of team leadership, members are disturbed by leaders who are unwilling to deal directly and effectively with self-serving or noncontributing team members."[1]

Consider that even though your team was chronically annoyed by this person and relieved at his departure, they may be slightly concerned by your having had enough chutzpah to actually do it. They won't be truly worried unless they think you will see them as yet more ROTTEN FRUIT(46). They will admire you, because you have shown yourself to be a manager who is capable of taking DIRECT ACTION(19).

Therefore:
It's time to pluck the rotten fruit and drop it in the dirt. Perhaps with the right fertilizer, he will grow into a fruit-bearing tree. Even though you are concerned about resources, making a move early prevents having to make hefty payments down the line. It is a guarantee that this person has a big problem either with you or with everyone. Depending on how you feel about the person, you may want to move him into a more appropriate group setting,

---

1. McConnell, Steve (1996). *Rapid Development,* Redmond, WA: Microsoft Press, 291.

move him to the role of solo contributor, or in extremis, invite him to leave the company.

It's better to set BACKFIRES(44) early to deal with this so that it ends up being a simple reassignment rather than appearing as punishment, but as a manager you probably are going to have fire someone sooner or later.

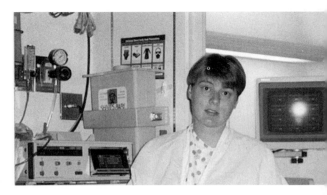

Separation anxiety.

47

Featurectomy

. . . in the human body, a useless little bit of tissue is found attached at the coupling of the large and small bowels—it is called the appendix. The appendix can become obstructed, causing swelling and intense pain. If not removed, it can burst, and the contents of the bowels will flow into the abdominal area. This can be a highly serious condition for the sufferer, resulting in infection and even death.

Software engineering projects often become confused, behind schedule, or hopelessly derailed because of unanticipated feature additions and changes that affect the project scope. Because of a lack of understanding of how a software system is designed, many clients don't understand the unreasonable burden that last-minute changes and additions can incur.

Photograph by Robin Seidner, © 1994. All rights reserved.

When a project is being scoped out between the project manager and the customer, quite often the customer will present a very high-level vision for the application. Consider the dot-com startup that had a big idea—WeAreGonna-BeHuge.com (WAG-BE). WAG-BE knew that its killer app was intended for a web-based browser and generally what the input and output should be. It knew that it would need a database "of some sort" and that whatever the outcome was, it should be better than the competition's tool. WAG-BE had a collection of features that must be included!

WAG-BE took its idea to the project manager at WeAreSlick (WAS) Engineering, who was more than happy to contract the work—this was a big job and WAG-BE wanted WAS to do it all over the next three months to a year. This particular WAS manager, Michael, did not employ PUSH THE CUSTOMER(26) because of the company's recklessly aggressive targets. The team members found themselves faced with a project for which no serious functional designing had been done, no concept of the back-end system requirements existed, and the completely useless management team at WAG-BE had no internal agreement on basic, yet defining issues. What they did have was an e-mail with a list of concepts that WAG-BE felt were absolutely required for the release of its tool.

Michael was stumped. He had his team write functional specifications with no knowledge of the user, design an object model for retrieving invalid data, and even choose an application server platform based on absolutely no criteria. Each artifact would be accepted for approximately one week, and then each attempt was summarily rejected as lacking the complete functionality. Even more frustrating, there always seemed to be changes introduced at each weekly meeting that would contradict some other area of functionality already defined. WAG-BE finally terminated the contract and did its best to blackball WAS throughout the industry. WAG-BE, itself, ultimately lost the confidence of its funding community by spending one million dollars with nothing but a bunch of Power Point decks to show for it. WAG-BE was floating belly-up within six months.

This project never had a chance, because neither the customer nor the manager ever took the time to define the true purpose of the application beyond a crazy list of features. It was the opinion of one of the developers on the WAS development team that the project could actually have been pushed live with only two weeks of serious development on the front end and the same on the back end! WAG-BE could have proven its ability to execute and could have learned more about its market through a prerelease of the system. Yet WAG-BE was obsessed with its list of high-level features—features with no purpose that it could ever cogently describe, nor from which it could part, if only temporarily, until a future release.

Like any customer making a huge purchase, it was natural for WAG-BE to ask for all it could get for its money. Without a working knowledge of software design, it is actually a bit much to expect a customer to understand that it is asking for a two-year project to be completed in six months. That is your job—the job of the manager for the software development team to define. You are about to expose your developers to a new project and ask them to perform, sometimes dramatically, within a fixed amount of time. And to your customer, a button is just a button, and data is just stuff. Everything else in the middle is just magic.

After a bit of customer reeducation, you will either lose the contract to someone like WAS or have a much smarter and more manageable customer. Knowing that they all walk in with a feature list either in their heads or in their notebooks, start looking at the customer-desired features. Work with the customer to determine which features are *absolutely required, next release, nice to have,* or *ridiculous.* Throughout an iterative process, you can use your own experience and the experience of a few of your developers to determine the development load the developers are incurring.

Too many up-front features will clog the development process, when infrastructure is being designed and constructed. A good design enables quick turnaround on future feature development, but features shouldn't affect the basic premises upon which the system was originally designed. This approach allows development cycles to be shorter and gives the customer the opportunity to quickly, yet organically, grow its system to meet its needs. Over time the customer will discover that many of its desires have changed from that original list because many of its assumptions were just flat wrong. Shorter cycling of a project provides more checkpoints with the customer.

Therefore:
Strike or defer useless and distracting features from the project plan. Instead, iterate the releases more frequently, ensuring that developers will concentrate on full and complete delivery of the most important system components, and that the customer ultimately receives full functionality in a more solid system.

A containment building for a 12-inch shell, or a photographer. Theodor Horydczak in gun breach of 12-inch C.A.C. Barbatt carriage gun at Fort Baker, California.

48

Containment Building

. . . the final line of defense if the safeguards fail is the containment building; a large, often dome-shaped structure that surrounds the reactor steam-producing equipment, and safety systems.[1]

◆◆◆

Your project is failing. You still think you can save it.

Maybe your project was destined to fail from the beginning owing to ridiculous scheduling, failure to engage in OVERTIME DETOX(23), or any combination

Photograph by Theodor Horydczak, taken sometime between 1920 and 1950; Library of Congress, Prints & Photographs Division, Theodor Horydczak Collection [LC-H822-T-1719 DLC].

1. United States Nuclear Regulatory Commission, 2000. *A Short History of Nuclear Regulation, 1946–1999.* http://www.nrc.gov/SECY/smj/shorthis.htm.

of reasons beyond your control. You see no gain, short- or long-term, if you FALL ON THE GRENADE(51), and it's too early to ABANDON SHIP(52).

Much criticism is directed toward the project, its staff, and its leadership. Despite all the visibility and concern, not one thing can be done to alleviate the pressure. Your repeated requests for resources, or adjustments to schedule, or a FEATURECTOMY(47) were rebuffed with such comforting aphorisms as "Work smarter, not harder," and "You're just not being creative enough!" This is a high profile project and cannot be easily scrapped without massive political fallout. If there is any hope of completing the project, the team must be kept intact.

Look around at other projects. Could this become part of something else? Is there a fast climber in your management chain who would love to add to his empire? Is the scent of reorganization apparent? Can you help slip your project into another context, with perhaps another layer of reporting as a shield?

This is sneaky and insidious, but it is a reasonable strategy that can work without any great ethical transgressions. Containment buildings are built around nuclear reactors to contain disasters such as leaks and meltdowns, preventing radiation from altering the gene pool of the cows that graze and the people that picnic nearby. But given the infectious destruction to morale that can spread if not contained through bureaucratic or other means, a CONTAINMENT BUILDING(48) is exactly what you require. The idea is to have the CONTAINMENT BUILDING(48) in place before the meltdown occurs. If no meltdown occurs, no harm is done. If it does, then your other projects, and your career, won't suffer any unwelcome mutations.

It may be necessary to enlist the help of others in the organization to effect such a strategic move, although you may not need to reveal the ultimate purpose of disaster avoidance. The idea is to keep your team, and you, together under a larger umbrella so that you can do something useful to stave off a terrible incident. A move like this appears as a reorganization, when in fact absolutely nothing but the organizational charts themselves have changed, as similarly proposed in CARGO CULT(49). Sheltered from direct scrutiny and filtered through the layers of reporting that have been added or obfuscated, the still-intact team can find the breathing room it needs to rebuild morale, redirect, and recover.

Therefore:
Fold the failing project into another, larger project, changing its name, if required, and apparently altering its scope. Accept, furthermore, that this can be a very dangerous thing to do.

◆◆◆

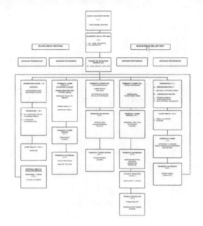

An organizational chart.

49

Cargo Cult

. . . Cargo cults have as their objective the betterment of traditional groups through the acquisition of Western technology, goods, and wealth through magic means. They are often messianic or millenarian in character, prophesying a future event that must be prepared for in advance. When that event does not take place, the cult usually subsides, sometimes to resurface under new circumstances.[1]

You have a project in trouble. Because you have run out of reasonable options, you are considering something radical.

There is a lot of attention being paid to your project these days. Criticism is directed at the project, its staff, and your leadership. People on the project are getting

1. Easton, Mark (1991, Jan. 1). *Papua New Guinea: Chapter 3. Postindependence.* Countries of the World.

beaten up with rumor and external interference, and you are constantly laboring over new plans. Team morale is deteriorating rapidly.

During World War II, airplanes arrived in New Guinea full of cargo, a portion of which was distributed to the indigenous New Guinean people. After the war, the planes stopped coming with their badly needed materials. In a state of heightened anxiety, some tribes built mockups of airplanes, hangars, and even a bamboo control tower that they hoped could bring back the planes and all the wealth that accompanied them. The people who participated in this ritual felt that their former good fortune was a direct result of the deities' good will and that the loss of goods indicated some sort of sin. If the proper rituals were performed, then the wealth would again be forthcoming.

In the office park and cubicle tribes, the major ritual practice among cultists is called *reorganization*. Instead of communal meals and spirit possession, the adherents experience a type of visual hallucination over a piece of paper called an *organizational chart*. The organic nature of the organizational chart is an object of power and inspiration among the believers. The magic is that nothing actually needs to change in the real world so long as the organizational chart shapes shift and alter alignment. The belief among those who practice such worship is that by altering the image of an organization on paper it will, in its earthly manifestation, alter itself accordingly.

In one large technology company, a software development organization some 1600 strong was "restructured" without warning from a deep, deep hierarchy into a flat, team-based, matrix-managed one. Nothing really changed; the deep hierarchy functionally remained, but no one was permitted to articulate the facts of its shape. Two things were accomplished by this. First, it could be declared that the organization was flat, more collaborative, and facile. Second, nothing really had to change, and no one's true power was threatened. Of course, once conditions deteriorated to the point that it was time for heads to roll, the organizational charts were reintroduced. This constituted a fundamental restructuring in official discussions, but it simply approximated what had been in place all along. Following the publication of the "new" organizational structure, there were some 6 reorganizations in 18 months, with the charts changing each time. Never did the powers nor the loyalties ever actually change.

Real reorganizations are hard. Moving names around and redrawing boxes and arrows, on the other hand, are easy and fun. Have some fun.

Earl Long, former governor of Louisiana, understood this power. When confronted by legislation that prevented him from serving a subsequent term as governor in 1952, Long ran and was elected as lieutenant governor instead, with a willing and subservient crony in the governor's slot. Long still ran things, although bureaucratically he was the number two man. In a sense, he just changed the organizational chart, for all the difference it made. Of course, everyone in Louisiana also understood this. Fortunately for you, many people in your organization may not. By the way, because it was not a subsequent term, Long was elected to the governorship again in 1956 and had to issue new organizational charts accordingly.

A paper reorganization might get critics off your back or buy a little more time. Possibly with the help of a sympathetic boss, redraw the organizational chart, publish it, and let the confusion, anger, amazement, and political intrigue obscure the real outcome, which is of course that no real change at all was made. Usually, those Machiavellians most enamored of organizational charts are the very people whom you need to tie up for a while as they try to determine how to scavenge the most benefit from the apparent shift of power.

Therefore:
Redraw the organizational charts. You might take the opportunity to pluck some ROTTEN FRUIT(46) anyway, and that serves as the perfect sacrificial project lamb and excuse for your machinations. Other than the charts, don't change a thing.

Official White House photo-graph of President William Jefferson Clinton, 1992.

50

Cop a Plea

. . . William Jefferson Clinton, and many others before him, could have avoided a deep pile of trouble had they just come right out and admitted up front that they had indeed done the wrong thing. Instead, each learned the hard way that the best defense is not obfuscation and denial, but rather blunt confrontation.

Sometimes a manager is called to task for blatant failure, mistakes, or things left undone. The accuser may well be correct in his or her assessment, but the motive for exposing a manager may be more insidious.

You have to be exceedingly careful sometimes. Everyone is vulnerable at one time or another, and although you might shun politics with the ease of SWITZER-LAND(6), by being a manager you are neck deep in them, like it or not. You may well have enemies who would trip you up to better their own situations. You may have a boss who views you as a threat and would like to whack you directly off the ladder in your climb through the organization. Of course, you may well have just screwed up somewhere and will be called to task on it. Naturally, you'd like to know how to defend yourself.

No defense can sometimes be the best defense. Recalling the travails of President Clinton, one cannot help but remember the declaration, "I did not have sexual relations with that woman, Ms. Lewinsky." Videotaped words to haunt a person eternally, those are. Never mind that *technically* he was telling the truth; after all, Special Prosecutor Kenneth Starr's own definition of sexual relations did not include fellatio, but we think that Good Ol' Bill was being TOO CLEVER BY HALF(15). You see, being technically correct only inflamed the whole affair, on all sides, and—let's face it—in politics you want to win hearts and minds, in that order. President Clinton, ordinarily a very savvy politician, got the order reversed this important time, and it blew up in his face.

The alternative? Well, imagine if Bill had immediately confronted his persecutors as he wagged his finger, "Yes, I had sexual relations with that woman, Ms. Lewinsky." There would have been an uproar of righteous indignation from all the hypocrites and purveyors of morality. We like to believe, that in the main, Mr. Clinton would have completely deprived the dogs at his heels of any further pretext for trying to drag him down. He was accused, he confessed, and he wasn't going to play the game any more.

Let's say you just agreed to let your best programmer go on vacation for a couple of weeks during a particularly tight crunch in your development schedule. Let's also pretend that your mortal enemy has noted this and in the weekly staff meeting makes mention of it, putting you on the spot for a judgment call that will not be looked upon favorably by some in higher positions. Your enemy's real intent, more than exposing your act, is to make you squirm and demean you further by your own obvious attempts at justifying what has been done. Even if you can fully and honestly explain the reasoning behind your decision, doing so will just play into the evil one's hands. Given this scenario, which is better: to carefully explain that your programmer had planned this vacation for 16 months and was reuniting with family from Sri Lanka, Chile, Burkina Faso, and Borneo, or to stand up and say, "Yes. I approved it. Absolutely."

By being blunt you may end the discussion right then and there. If you are further challenged, think of how the two of you will be viewed as you reluctantly reveal the facts that fed your decision. By immediately taking full responsibility, you have put the ball back in your nemesis's court. If he should choose to press further, you will only look better as you let him demonstrate the venality of his attack. You offered to end the squabble right off by making a full disclosure. If you are pursued, whatever gains this bestowed on your enemy will be eroded with each further interrogation. Emotionally, you will be the victor. At worst, you will have admitted bad judgment, and admissions of errors, particularly when they were made for good reasons, are always a net gain in the long run. That's just the way humans are.

Therefore:
Be forthright. It's not the crime; it's the cover-up that gets you.

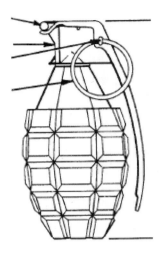

The obsolete MK2 fragmenta-
tion hand grenade

51

Fall on the Grenade

. . . projects have problems. Sometimes when problems loom large, people
either completely deny what is occurring or unearth someone who can be
blamed for what is going wrong. Denial and blame are ineffective leadership
devices. When you are the leader, you are expected to defend your team from
disorder and ruin.

Sometimes, despite your best efforts, problems threaten the lifeblood of the
entire project. Your developers may be producing splendid works of code, but
luck, bad decisions, fate, or some unseen hand can intervene and drive a sig-
nificantly destructive event that can threaten to completely collapse your
project.

U.S. Army Field Manual FM 3-23.30, GRENADES AND PYROTECHNIC SIGNALS, *01 Sep*
2000, Appendix E, Figure E-3.

When things start to go sour, senior management has a knack for smelling it out. Rather than letting you use DIRECT ACTION(19), they will begin to pressure you for more detailed and frequent updates on the project. They'll insult you, badger you, and subtly accuse you of incompetence. You can feel it when you walk in to each directors' meeting. And you don't need this sort of trouble. You've been around the block a few times, and you know there are many ways by which you can cover your posterior just fine. Find a sacrificial lamb, some weaker manager, and throw him to the wolves. Or, you could be proactive and run screaming to management about how you've been completely screwed over by this or that and how it is outside of your control. Your customers will hate you, and your developers will see you as impotent and sooner or later desert you. Even your seniors will see you for what you are—they will allow you to proceed with your ruse only because, frankly, they recognize themselves in your actions. After all, you're a manager—you know it's possible to go years without being *directly* responsible for a thing.

Lately, you've been working to build your credibility with your engineers and don't want to lay waste to all that effort. Your career is looking sound and healthy with your conscience mostly intact—there is clearly more at risk than just this project. This quandary is a live grenade ready to explode. And as a leader with TOTAL COMMITMENT(2), you may have only one option: Throw yourself on it. Save those around you. Take full and complete responsibility for this problem. Sacrifice yourself for the good of the team. You'll be a hero to your engineers, and other managers will drop their jaws in awe—although the foolish among them will be plotting with glee, thinking of how your empire will be added to theirs.

Ernest H. Shackleton was a British explorer of the Antarctic who led the Trans-Antarctic Expedition from 1914 to 1917. Shackleton and his team planned to cross the Antarctic continent, crossing the South Pole—a feat of great historical and scientific value. In what many still feel is one of the most incredible adventures of this sort, the *Endurance* left England for the Antarctic. Unfortunately, winter set in early, and the ship became solidly frozen into the ice, drifting at the mercy of the ice floes. Shackleton wrote in his journal, "If I had guessed a month ago that the ice would grip us here, I would have established our base at one of the landing places at the great glacier. But there seemed no reason to anticipate that the fates would prove unkind. . . ."[1] After months of being trapped in the ice and drifting more than 1000

---

1. Found on http://www.south-pole.com/p0000098.htm, "Antarctic Explorers: Ernest Shackleton."

miles, the sternpost finally buckled and twisted under the force of an ice floe. The crew was forced to abandon ship.

Shackleton moved his crew to the ice floe as they watched the *Endurance* sink to the bottom of the sea. Hauling three 20-foot boots with them and as much of their stores as possible, the crew of 28 was left drifting with the winds. They ultimately made their way to Elephant Island, where Shackleton immediately laid plans for an 800-mile voyage across the stormy ocean to South Georgia, south of Cape Horn, in one of the little boats accompanied by a crew of 5. Departing in a blizzard and traveling at a rate of three miles per hour, the tiny boat and its small crew fought massive waves, wore soaked clothes, and slept in water-logged sleeping bags to finally arrive at the cliffs of South Georgia. The men were miles from a whaling station on the island, separated by 5000 feet of mountains and glaciers.

Frostbitten and with matted hair and torn clothes that had been on their backs for more than a year, they finally reached the station. Immediately a rescue mission to Elephant Island was planned. After three unsuccessful attempts, Shackleton managed to reach the island on the fourth attempt. After 105 days on Elephant Island the crew was discovered. Shackleton wrote, "[W]e had entered [the Antarctic] a year and a half before with well-found ship, full equipment, and high hopes. We had 'suffered, starved and triumphed, groveled down yet grasped at glory, grown bigger in the bigness of the whole.' We had seen God in His splendours, heard the text that Nature renders. We had reached the naked soul of man."[2] Miraculously, every member of the crew survived.

Acts of courage are in short supply among managers, and we concede that it is a difficult path to follow. Shackleton did not parse the problems, assign particular blame, and extract himself neatly and nicely. He jumped in with both feet at every stage. We are reminded of Harry S. Truman: *The Buck Stops Here.* Yes, it does have to stop somewhere, and, frankly, it is a rare bird who can say, without equivocation, "I am responsible."

> Therefore:
> When problems arise on your project team, don't waste precious cycles hunting down someone to blame. Take responsibility for solving the problem yourself, or stand up and take the heat when the problem is unrecoverable. Then, move on.

---

2. Ibid.

Of course, you could avoid having to do this by lighting some preemptive BACK-FIRES(44). However, when necessary, being seen as someone who steps into the breach when others would cower and who will risk eviscerating himself to protect his team by falling on the grenade, gives amazing power to you in the long run. The grenade you fall on may turn out to be a dud, but your gesture will awe those around you anyway.

Under the steady hand of Captain Robert E. Hudgins, this one made it back to port in one piece. Not the Titanic, to be sure, since the Titanic is at the bottom of the Atlantic.

52

Abandon Ship

. . . *the 46-ton* Titanic *was designed to be a two-compartment ship, which meant that it was subdivided into 16 watertight compartments by 15 transverse bulkheads. In case of emergency, the captain could flip a switch on the bridge, which closed the watertight doors in the bulkhead and thereby allowed the ship to stay afloat if even two consecutive compartments were destroyed. Captain Smith piloted the ill-fated RMS* Titanic, *known as the "sinking palace," which went down in April 1912. Questions remain as to why the iceberg warnings went ignored. More than 1500 people drowned or froze to death in the icy water.*

◆◆◆

Despite your best-laid plans, a good budget, and a solid project team, it has become obvious that sinking failure awaits your software development project. There is nothing that can be done to prevent a tragedy.

From the collection of Carol Stimmel.

There are variables and people that are outside the sphere of influence of even the most assertive and attentive managers. Despite your warnings and flag raising, for some reason upper management is still pressing the project forward, perhaps even presenting this as a flagship project. Late into the evening, your developers are working frantically on a project that you know is taking on water. This will be a disaster when the bow finally dips below the surface; your developers will be devastated with yet another wasted effort, and your superiors will mark you as ineffective. You will be the last one standing on deck when the ship finally goes under.

You may feel much like Captain Smith when he discovered that, despite his special orders to change course to avoid ice, an iceberg had sheared off 250 feet of his vessel. Water rushed into five of the watertight compartments, and the ship could stay afloat for only another hour or two. Apparently, his wireless operator had neglected to report to the bridge that ice lay directly in front of the ship, leaving off reporting it to the bridge until he had completed several personal transmissions for the wealthy and influential passengers.

Depending on the nature of your organization, you may discover that issues of company protocol and de facto regulation are standing in your way. On the *Titanic*, regulations on the number of lifeboats was based on tonnage of the vessel instead of the actual number of passengers. Therefore, there were only 16 lifeboats and 4 collapsible lifeboats for more than 2500 passengers.

The ultimate goal is not to go down with the ship, but it may be what is required of you in the end if no lifeboat returns. What happens if you put the short-term goals of your career above the long-term effects of making the right decision for your development team and your company? Killing a project is never an easy choice.

Your judgment will be questioned, and you may be branded as a quitter, a Chicken Little, or a Cassandra. Your very security, emotionally and professionally, is at risk. Deepak Chopra, in *The Seven Spiritual Laws of Success,* reminds us:

> The search for security is an illusion . . . the search for security and certainty is actually an *attachment* to the known. And what's the known? The known is our past. The known is nothing other than the prison of past conditioning. There's no evolution in that—absolutely none at all. And when there is no evolution, there is stagnation, entropy, disorder, and decay.[1]

---

1. Chopra, Deepak (1994). *The Seven Spiritual Laws of Success.* San Rafael, CA: Amber-Allen Publishing and New World Library, 86.

You may have missed early opportunities to bail out your ship, but you know you are going down now. Don't take your team with you if you know you won't come up again.

We know many software developers who at some point in their career have seen themselves subject to the whimsy of huge corporate mergers and less-than-friendly takeovers. The unchallenged illusion of unsinkable concepts, products, and companies fueled the recent dot-bomb spectacle. In the wake of these back-of-the-envelope deals, you can find many *Titanic*s captained by a plethora of middle managers that are choking on seawater.

These are opportunities to stand up and holler "Abandon Ship!!"

Therefore:
Free your developers to the lifeboats of other projects by constructing the high-tech version of an SOS message for ships floating nearby. You need to start working your colleagues for opportunities for your team, creating new ones, or promising to serve as an excellent reference when the ship finally sinks. Let your team know that it is not a dishonorable thing for them to leave either your team or the company.[2]

Remember the depth of humanity that it takes to lead with TOTAL COMMITMENT(2). This may have required you to PUSH THE CUSTOMER(26) or to FALL ON THE GRENADE(51). Self-sacrifice often pays off if you can be patient enough to allow the cycles to complete themselves.

---

2. We understand that if you're a true Machiavellian, you'll push this off on some underling whom you don't like or who is ambitious to the point of being a threat to you. Then you look like a nice, delegating sort of boss, and when the ship goes down, you're safely slurping down slices of mango and looking for the next rescue ship from your metaphoric tropical island.

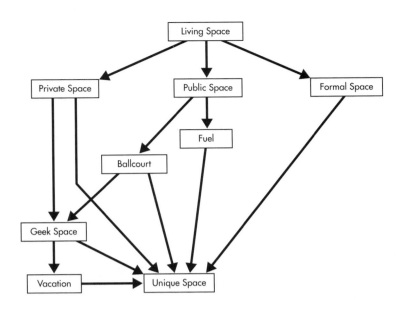

Environmental Patterns

The patterns in this section are about what surrounds your developers, including the supply of fuel to body and soul. Though idealized in some respects, they are not beyond realization and may be the easiest and most direct ways of improving the morale of teams. The walls that surround developers do influence their behavior and productivity, something which modular office designers must have taken into account only after considering capital cost, uniformity, and the apparent virtue of utter blandness.

On the island of Santorini, gracious living abounds.

53

Living Space

. . . imagine the physical world of the software developer as it is defined by three-and-a-half walls arranged at right angles to each other and the floor to form what is universally referred to as a "cube." Inside, modular, laminate units form bookshelves, file cabinets, desk, and workspace. There might be a plastic sliding tray to hold pens and pencils, little shelves for a memento or two, a tape dispenser, and a stapler. The monitor is held at an average optimal height, and the keyboard and chair are ergonomically integrated, adjustable, and balanced to reduce repetitive stress injuries. The colors of the cloth walls are a muted cranberry or perhaps a pearlescent gray.

Will software developers ever be able to shape their environment to fit the mixture of solitary and collaborative work that they do? Is it possible to have a workspace that reflects the lives and desires of the people who use it, that

Photograph by Leah Rogers, date unknown. Used by permission.

surrounds them in such comfort that they are freed from any environmental tensions that hamper their work?

Modern offices, the world of the cube, are institutional nightmares. Just as developers want to scream every time some process geek tries to jam their creative impulses into the nice little boxes of the Software Engineering Institute (SEI) model, why should they feel any different when they are physically shoved into uniformly bland, utilitarian cells? The cells do not offer privacy from the ambient noise and intrusions of the office, nor do they easily accommodate the fluid social interactions that facilitate the natural development process.

"There is not a crumb of dirt anywhere, nor a chair misplaced. We are all alone here and we are dead."[1]

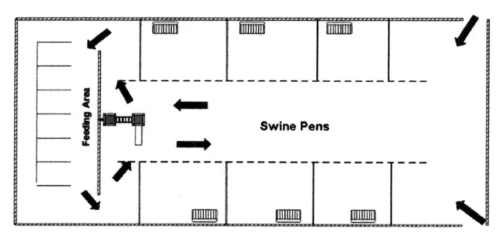

The kernel of an idea in office design.

---

1. Miller, Henry (1961). *Tropic of Cancer.* New York: Grove Press, 1.

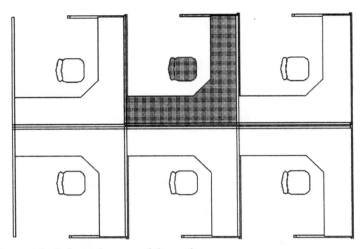

The grayed-out cube belonged to one of the authors.

As developers ourselves, we feel a little ungrateful to be complaining about our cubes when we consider that we are making decent salaries with reasonable benefits, personal days, and, well, to be honest, most of us aren't really fit to do anything else. Those of us with enough gray hairs think back to earlier times when engineering offices might be huge bays flooded with unforgiving and unflattering fluorescent lighting. There every time you went to the toilet it could be easily noted:

> When I started as an engineer in the late 1950s, they put us all in this gigantic hangar, in which there were rows and rows of drafting tables lined up. The more senior you were, the further back you sat in this arrangement. On my first day, after orientation and all the admin stuff, they marched me into the hangar from the rear. As we walked down the aisle almost every engineer's head lifted from its table and watched.[2] It felt like I was going to the gallows. After what seemed like an eternity, we arrived at the very first row. As the new guy, I was assigned the leftmost

---

2. The use of the pronoun "its" in reference to the heads of the engineers is intentional. Up in the hierarchy of many companies, engineers are counted as "heads." Heads are faceless and interchangeable. Heads are easily fractionalized and therefore useful in computation of "resources," which is another word that removes the humanity from the person of the engineer. Might as well refer to engineers collectively as "the equipment."

drafting table in that row. Behind me sat every person who was a superior to me, able to watch every move—when I came in, when I went to the can, when I took lunch, even when my head wasn't down over my work. It was intimidating, to say the least.[3]

So perhaps the cubic life *is* an improvement. After all, isn't death by strangulation an improvement over death by slow roasting over an open fire?

Stockyards, Chicago.

Office designers are under great pressure to provide the *idea* of private office space without incurring the costs of building for such space. Yet, opposing the idea of private office space is the fact that much of software development work is collabo-

---

Photograph by John Vachon, 1941; Library of Congress, Prints & Photographs Division, FSA-OWI Collection [LC-USF34-063124-D DLC].

3. Oral history from Eugene T. Beasley, Ph.D., as told to one of the authors.

rative and requires larger, configurable spaces to shape to the work teams. Although the intentions are honorable, the compromise between these two has led to a situation in which the spaces are neither private nor configurable. Furthermore, such amenities as refrigerators, microwaves, soft drink and snack machines, lunch tables, and the other items that help sustain geeks at work seem never to be in spaces that are amenable to relaxation and renewal. In the case of one particular office, the only accessible place for the soft drink machine was directly next to the room where all the dog and pony shows occurred for the company suits—and the only convenient way in or out was through that conference room. Developers could be spotted peeking through the movable walls to see if they could sneak through for a pop, or if they had to walk the entire circumference of the building to go in the back way.

It is a rare office environment that has a flow among its spaces, and the transitions are often harsh. Typically, as an afterthought, whatever space is left over, whether an existing, fully walled office or some dismal corner of the building, is used to stuff everything that doesn't blend with the color scheme of the carpeted cubicle walls. Stepping from the cool, sound-deadened, numbing world of the cubes into a break room starkly lit with an ice machine crunching away, a refrigerator groaning, scratched 1970s linoleum glaring, filled with rigid chairs and cheap folding tables with fake wood veneer does nothing to scrape off the tensions of a debugging session gone bad. Even in trendy Silicon Valley operations, many of the best designs fall victim to overcrowding and spreading workspaces into inhospitable areas of the building—next to the elevator or into an insurance company's abandoned storeroom. Given that too often people are spending more waking hours at the office than in their own homes, why do we insist on putting them in such manifestly uninhabitable spaces?

Have you ever wondered why people who have home offices rarely emulate the cube? In fact, have you ever wondered why offices in homes rarely really look like offices, and why even the most driven workaholic does not have a home that looks like your office spaces? When people gather socially, what sort of place attracts them? Why is it that despite the vast studies devoted to optimizing and perfecting office environments and the huge success of the modular office manufacturers, most of us prefer working from home when we can, and that within the limits of our little cubes we persist in making home-like touches? Why do we insist on decorating our external cube walls with articles, art, and other items such as waterfalls and fake windows? Is there something going on here that perhaps you should consider when choosing office space? Is it possible that the ordinary house is a model better adapted to the nature of software development than anything else yet devised?

Christopher Alexander wrote in *A Pattern Language:*

> Though these spaces were designed to support family life, they turn out also to support the natural structure of work groups: there are small spaces for private and half-private offices, slightly larger spaces for work groups of two to six, usually one space where 12 people can gather, and a commons centered around the kitchen and dining room. Furthermore, within each space there are usually a variety of walls, half-walls, window seats, which allow for changes within the rooms.[4]

It is probably going through your mind that the expense of such an endeavor is far too much to bear. You can't possibly move a 100-person development operation to your grandma's basement! However, given that the single greatest cost in the production of quality software is the labor to produce it, what are you buying if you save a few bucks in the setup of the environment only to lose it in subtle but expensive ways because no one really enjoys being there?

Other issues, such as zoning, intrude and often preclude the choice of actual houses for commercial use. This and much more is addressed by Alexander in *A Pattern Language*. He takes on the much more ambitious and important issues of whole communities and the integration of work, life, and play. We simply cannot delve into all that here, lacking time, space, and talent, and strongly insist that you read Alexander's book. However, even taking these issues into account, the family house is an excellent model for a workspace that really works, and you could adapt it to other models in your office plan.

> What is comfort design? Corner windows reserved for communal spaces with couches, rather than for offices for vice presidents. Any wall that can be made serpentine or tipped at an angle is better than a straight, flat wall. The interior surfaces of a building may be ripped away, exposing ducts, brick, rough timber.[5]

Wouldn't you love to have a sofa or two around, a coffee table, some end tables, a few comfy chairs, and lighting from a few funky incandescent lamps with a few halogen spots for reading? Wouldn't it be nice to have an informal gathering, as

---

4. Alexander, Christopher (1977). *A Pattern Language.* New York: Oxford University Press, 692.
5. Bronson, Po (1999). *The Nudist on the Late Shift.* New York: Random House, 218.

described in PUBLIC SPACE(57), where it is possible to discuss technical solutions to a tough problem? If *you* would like it, we imagine your developers would love it.

> Therefore:
> Make offices as close to the shape and ambiance of personal dwellings as possible. If at all possible, actually make houses or apartment buildings into your office space. Create what amounts to a home, a true Living Space that can be given as is to your developers to be shaped by them into an environment that they feel natural in, and within which they can move and think and work and interact.

There is an important need for both PRIVATE SPACE(56) and PUBLIC SPACE(57) and even space for play, such as a BALL COURT(55).

An uncommon place, where
one could relax . . . or jump.

54

Unique Place

. . . many creative people seem to respond best to new stimuli and to new environments, and without them they quickly become weary. Emptiness, boredom, and irritability soon follow.

Skilled software developers will leave a place of employment at the slightest provocation, especially those who live in the high-tech areas of the country where venture-funded companies arrive overnight to raid and pillage the best developers. One sniff of impending boredom or an askance look from a corporate officer and they are out the door. How do you keep the good ones around?

Many stay for money, others for options, and even some for stability, benefit packages, and free soda pop, but the motivated, creative talents stay only if the work is engaging and interesting. If you desire the sharpest developers and the most enthusiastic input, you need to shape your company environment into one that inspires creativity. It is a unique place today in which developers can really innovate, yet the environment may be paramount in nurturing that ability. Not to allow the developer's mind to break free is to risk losing your best talent and engendering discontent:

> When employees are not passionate about what they do on a daily basis, work can become repetitive, boring, and possibly meaningless. This kind of feeling is hardly conducive to creative thinking. Humans are born to create. When the creative spirit is restrained, it fights back with negativity, lack of motivation, and disrespect. This creates a breeding ground for corporate toxicity.[1]

Start with the physical space. Look around you: A dried out building with 25-year-old chairs and chipped vt3270 terminal desks simply doesn't convey the kind of environment that anyone would want to work in. What do your meeting rooms look like? Are your best and brightest condemned to writing on little flip charts? Does your company ration the pens and enforce the use of those cheap ballpoints? Can a developer turn on some music or yell an obscenity without fear of a Human Resources repercussion? How about color? A lot of beige, gray, and other neutral tones? Yuck.

Consider innovative ways to make your workplace unique by offering added value to your developers that will make them want to stay. Ask your developers what would make your company a nice place to be. In congested areas of the country, this could mean allowing telecommuting a few days a week to relieve the stress of commute. It may mean building a BALL COURT (55), or providing an onsite masseuse periodically (that *you* pay for). How about running an entertaining movie on the breakroom televisions? Don't forget the popcorn. Make it fun to be your employee. We know about companies that provide onsite breast exams (okay, not fun, but definitely useful), while another leased BMWs for all their developers during a stellar year. Be imaginative and find out what will make your company unique and something to brag about.

Get rid of cubes as discussed in PRIVATE SPACE(56), PUBLIC SPACE(57), and GEEK SPACE(58); nix the rules against having a keg every now and then, and

---

1. DeSalvo, Tina (1999, June 1). Unleash the creativity in your organization. *HR Magazine.*

try to loosen up. We've even heard of a company having LEGO contests and a cheese construction day. Institute a team that deals with workplace issues, and help ensure that they are empowered with a budget and corporate buy-in to make your place *the place* to be.

If all this sounds prohibitively expensive, remember how much more expensive it is to hire new talent instead of keeping current talent around.

> Therefore:
> Construct an inspirational environment for your team. It should reflect the essence of your company, so ask the people inside your company so that you can learn what they would like to experience in their work environment. Discover the perks that will allow your developers to relax and enjoy themselves—where work is an opportunity to create with imaginative enthusiasm.

For other ideas, consider FUEL(60). Everyone's got to eat and drink well.

Basketball game at the annual field day of the FSA (Farm Security Administration) farm workers community, Yuma, Arizona, 1942.

55

Ball Court

. . . at the Wupatki National Monument in northern Arizona, United States, there is a ball court. Built around 1100 A.D., this exceptional structure had a purpose far greater than games. Archeologists believe that the court functioned as a link between remote regions and made Wupatki a desirable place to exchange goods and ideas and to breed amiability between people. Despite the difficulties of scratching out an existence in the high desert, the people still valued play.

Any job that requires the laborer to sit in solitude, inert, while staring at a glowing screen hour after hour, day after day, is exhausting. Not only can this stationary activity bring physical damage to the body, but it unquestionably inhibits creativity and normal social interaction between coworkers.

Photograph by Russell Lee, 1942; Library of Congress, Prints & Photographs Division, FSA-OWI Collection [LC-USF33-013274-M1 DLC].

Repetitive stress ailments are the most numerous of reported workplace ailments. This is not a surprise, especially to those of us whose paychecks are measured by the speed and efficiency with which we move our fingers across our keyboards. There are those of us who wear wrist splints or feel our funny bone pinch us daily and can picture ourselves snatching an ibuprofen[1] coupon from an old lady to medicate our strained eyes. For those of you who came from a different place (like some hot-shot business school), try to imagine this:

> You have been offered a job that will involve your standing upright in a corner with your arms held straight in front of you, hands dangling at the wrists, staring at a white square pasted to the wall. On the white square are logic problems. You solve them one by one, and when you discover an answer, you mark it in the appropriate place on the square. Every day a new set of problems for you to grapple with appears in the square. Sometimes the square will randomly fall off the wall, at which point you get a fresh white square with the exact same problems for you to recalculate— all of your work has been lost. Sounds grim, but the payoff could be huge! The only catch is, you have to do this for 8 to 10 hours a day in 4-year cycles, or until your options vest, which may or may not be worth anything.

Would you do it? Some of you are asking, "How many options?" Software developers do the analogous to this every day.

This is not an absurd made-for-television scenario, but a reality for millions of workers worldwide. Day after day our wrists hang suspended over a keyboard where we grapple with logical problems. Power failures or the "blue screen of death" intermittently erases our efforts—our work evaporates before our eyes. Unfortunately for our bodies, the only time we think to take a serious break is when our bladder finally forces us to the necessary facilities. (By the way, never stop a running developer.) At first, most of us notice the fatigue and shoulder pains. We compensate with our favorite painkiller, a splint on our wrists, or a new pair of magnifiers. But often, sitting in exactly the same position for decades, our bodies simply fail us; neuropathy, anxiety, and excruciating pain set in.

You may argue the point that it is not your job to care for the bodies of your software developers. After all, the company has provided them with every ergonomic

---

1. Ibuprofen is an over-the-counter analgesic that is more popular than aspirin among developers.

advantage. (Well, some companies have. Just a few years ago, while one of the authors was working for a multinational company, she could be found sitting at her old desk in a broken chair that flipped back dangerously if not propped exactly right.) We are concerned not only with the problems of physiology, but with the quality of our lives. If that concept doesn't interest you, then at least consider the creative give-and-take that is lost by tired, dazed, software developers who literally cannot formulate an understandable sentence after hours of hacking a problem in their little cubes. Lost creativity is lost potential and ultimately will drive the will and abilities of your team down the tubes. Creative give-and-take is the lifeblood of any high-performance team.

Keeping your software developers primed follows much the same process as the athlete; stay warm, stretch, limber up, and focus when it's time for your event. The demands of the developer, while primarily intellectual, take their toll on the body as well as on the mind. Find ways to stomp out the root causes of these problems before they become life-altering events. Interrupt the hours of enforced dormancy and maniacal overuse of a few small muscles with activities that don't require problem solving, deep thinking, small muscle involvement, or any electronic device.

Buy a used foosball[2] table at a yard sale, and throw it in the breakroom, or, if you have a discretionary fund, find an old pool table or Ping-Pong table. Cards can be a nice break and provide a little friendly competition. Or get an old mechanical arcade game that is totally unprofessional, but nonetheless fun. Rig it so it will run without tokens. You probably have a parking lot at your building, so haul out the roller blades and hockey sticks during lunch. The more coordinated among us will enjoy a basketball hoop or hackey sack.

The idea is to introduce activities that can be enjoyed with others and that will provide an opportunity for your team members to build relationships, talk about their kids, gloat about their latest acts of genius, and, most of all, exercise some long-neglected muscles. Encourage activities by organizing team competitions that are more exciting than the office baby pool. You can set up interteam competitions or simply concentrate on your own group. Of course, some people will be so happy in their isolation that you may need to drag them kicking and screaming to participate, so some trickery or brazen threats may be in order for them, while others may be frighteningly competitive and will need to be tempered somehow. Ultimately, you

---

2. A table version of European football or what is called soccer in America, the *foos* coming from the German *fuß*.

will encourage a more balanced daily regimen for brain and body and deepen the relationships among the people in your workplace.

> Therefore:
> Provide a way to break up the tediousness and isolation of the daily life of the software developer. Allow for activities during the workday that encourage friendly competition, unprofessional behavior, senseless frivolity, or just the chance to change scenery.

A BALL COURT(55) should always be a part of the PUBLIC SPACE(57).

Contemplating a sandwich on the Acropolis, Athens, Greece.

56

Private Space

. . . we discussed in LIVING SPACE(53) *why we should reject the physical construct of the modern software development environment—the "cube"—as the atomic unit of office space. However, if this model is abandoned, then it will be necessary to consciously construct certain private areas that may not organically develop on their own.*

People in any office configuration have a need for solitude, and this must be provided within the LIVING SPACE(53) so that employees can gain meaningful separateness when required for heightened concentration or for more personal matters.

In one office, a new mother was quietly retiring to the company's usability laboratory a few times a day to pump breast milk for her newborn baby. The room had

237

subdued lighting and a comfortable chair, so it was perfect. Because the door did not lock from the inside, while in the lab she would tape a sign on the door that said, simply, "Privacy Please." The lab was rarely used so this was not a problem, but on one occasion the vice president of the facility was giving a dog and pony show of the whiz-bang features in the building, one of which was, of course, the usability lab. Without even noticing the sign on the door, he flung open the door to be treated to a view of a double breast pump chugging away. If you have never witnessed this in person, this can be quite shocking as it sits on a large rolling metal stand and employs a significant electric motor. From then on out, she was asked to pump in the ladies room or the locker room. Of course, having to express your breasts while sitting on the toilet in the company rest room is unpleasant and hardly reflective of concern for family life. It certainly made a direct and negative impact on every woman and decent man in the company.

People scheduling medical procedures ought not need to whisper *colonoscopy* into their telephones or be required to answer detailed questions about the procedure for all to hear, such as, "Now, why did your doctor refer you here?" Similarly, those who are awaiting the results of some test should not have to fear their co-workers overhearing them as they explain to a receptionist that they are calling to discover their HIV status or the outcome of their sperm count. People buying or selling houses have a right to keep the particulars of their transactions private. Those communicating with accountants or brokers shouldn't disturb others with details of their wins, losses, or tax status. When someone's child is in trouble at school, it should be between the parent and the principal and the child, and not anyone else. If someone is having marital difficulties, should he be forced to share his travails with neighbors in the cube farm? Finally, people sometimes just need a place to which they can retreat for some quiet reflection.

If you dislike developers, we probably started annoying you two paragraphs back when we first climbed on this soapbox. After all, it's not your job to provide a phone for anyone scheduling personal appointments or conducting real estate transactions, never mind breast pumping. All the policy manuals clearly state that an employee should have no expectation of privacy in the workplace, and it's no secret that many companies monitor e-mail and track web site visits by their employees (see DEFENSE DE PISSER(24)). Your company may already be actively monitoring and reporting when, where, and what each user is doing with the corporate assets. Anybody who has ever had root password before knows that there is *no* reasonable expectation of privacy for the casual user in any company that relies on electronically mediated communication. The more clever among us may defend ourselves by encrypting e-mail communications, by storing data on disk, and by relying on a variety of cryptographic techniques, but it is impossible to work around all elements of the communications system, such as voice mail and incoming e-mail. Either way, any well-informed employee knows that the door is always open for the employer to monitor his communications.

So, it may be surprising that we posit that every software worker should have the freedom to make a private phone call, accomplish a web-based transaction, or check his or her personal e-mail at work, with the absolute expectation of freedom from probative action. We believe, however, that the issue is deeper, as it cuts to the quick of the relationship between employer and employee and a more productive work environment—the legitimate needs of both employee and employer. Issues of privacy in the workplace have traditionally revolved around this hallucinogenic concept *of the legitimate use of company resources*. Is it "legitimate" to make a bank transfer over the phone to cover the mortgage check? How about a personal phone call from the school nurse telling you that your child is sick and needs to go home? What about e-mail from a friend about a new treatment for the cancer you father has? In general, the "abuses" are fairly mild and do much to enable a smoother life for the "abuser."

Yes, there are true abusers of the system, and we do believe that a corporation has the right to protect its assets from some hack solving the next prime number and bringing down all the customer service computers or the rogue running his own FTP server off your laboratory box. These are rare exceptions. Electronic monitoring is strangely violate, as it assumes that we are all under suspicion of wrongdoing with no provocation for that thinking, as if wanting to know the results of a child's strep test somehow robs the company of its precious bodily fluids.

Failing to provide physically private space can be seen by some workers as an extension of these intrusions, as though management did this on purpose to exercise even greater control over people's private lives. Like drug testing (DEFENSE DE PISSER(24)), this points to lack of trust on the part of the leadership that presupposes malfeasance on the part of the employee and can therefore precipitate many unwanted side effects. Despite nearly universal corporate policies against private use of telephones and e-mail for personal business, this practice is itself nearly universal, and it's time to accept it. Forcing people to go offsite to handle sensitive business is not good policy as it interrupts the flow of the workday and increases the solitude between already chronically isolated employees.

Simple phone booths can be a workable solution for those needing to make private calls, and unmonitored terminals in kiosks that can be used to make web-based transactions or to check personal mail could be made available. A small living room area with a couch, a chair, a small television and radio, and a locking door could serve duty for nursing mothers and others requiring comfortable privacy to shake off a nagging headache. A private office or two that are open to anyone's use are also helpful. Place these away from high traffic areas to avoid drop-ins and unwanted noise.

> Therefore:
> Come to an agreement with your employees about what their reasonable expectations of privacy are and resolve how you can meet both them and the company's interests. Provide private space of various types. Allow your employees to proceed with their lives and to work in parallel for more productivity, less interruption, and a framework upon which to build trust between employer and employee.

Per Christopher Alexander, "In any building—house, office, public building, summer cottage—people need a gradient of settings which have different degrees of intimacy."[1] Hence we include PRIVATE SPACE(56), PUBLIC SPACE(57), and UNIQUE PLACE(54) in this work. Alexander's work goes much deeper and covers a far greater span of human architecture and it is highly recommended, but for the office these few patterns suffice as a large step to improving the typical work environment encountered today.

Photograph by Leah Rogers, date unknown. Used by permission.

---

1. Alexander, Christopher (1977). *A Pattern Language.* New York, Oxford University Press, 610.

Stoa of Attalos.

57

Public Space

. . . much of software development is solitary and contemplative. But there is also a great deal of collaborative effort, and such creative collectives occur in formal settings as well as informally in casual spaces. In the cube world, these informal spaces are typically hallways, landings, or just outside the cube of someone else trying to work on her own development. Developers need space in which to gab, speculate, air theories, and generally brainstorm without it always having to rain.

As part of software development LIVING SPACE(53), developers require informal gathering areas in which to relax and escape for a break. These spaces also have the advantage of providing a free-form environment in which technical conversations do not have to be directed but can spiral and loop back and stall and leap in the true nature of creative collaboration.

Too often in formally convened meetings, developers strike a vein of rich material in which the mining is not straightforward but requires some probing and exploring. At the first inkling that time may be "wasted" by such collaborative thought, the leader may ask the people involved to "take it offline" because the discussion is veering off the agenda as geeks get into some exciting riffing. Unfortunately, in many, if not most, companies, there is nowhere to really take such discussions, except within another meeting room, the use of which usually requires a reservation. Furthermore, if it's like every other meeting room we've encountered, it will be another airless, windowless, lifeless, sterile space. There's nowhere to sit casually or to lean back and stare up for inspiration. There is no room to stand and pace and wave one's arms and spin when inspiration strikes. The sort of chairs used in meeting rooms do not encourage people to literally put their heads together over a diagram. It isn't possible to sip thoughtfully at one's coffee and lean back to stare distantly into the implications of a theory held forth by another. Unlike our living rooms at home where we can get lively or quiet, or shift the furniture to fit our activity, meeting rooms permit only "professional" discussions, passionless recitation of previously recorded observations, fit into an agenda and within the time allotted in the company room scheduling software. The very nature of most meeting rooms makes people want to evacuate the room as soon as possible. When was the last time you experienced joy in such a space?

Public space also facilitates chance meetings and the exchange of information that may be extremely valuable to the recipient. Frequently, someone just stopping by to get a coffee or take a break will overhear this information. Nearby a spirited conversation may be in progress. Perhaps the interloper can be of help or may benefit from the overflow from the exchange.

New York City street life.

Something has been lost since we all moved into cubes with our powerful workstations and personal stereos. Back in the days of limited computers, terminals would all be clustered in a single room, and developers would share space while writing code or debugging. In one company, this arrangement had the side effect of promulgating bug fixes and new developments in the platform software on which everyone built. It also helped create a sort of living and informal directory of faces, so that before long no one was a complete stranger. Public space may help restore some of this incidental interaction.

> Therefore:
> Set aside some open space on the periphery for a couch, some chairs, a table, and other amenities conducive to relaxing a bit. Try to make the space somewhat intimate and casual so that people will tend to talk or at least acknowledge each other. Make it large enough to accommodate up to a dozen people or so, in one or more small groups, even at the same time.

Having public space complements PRIVATE SPACE(56) and is essential in creating a true LIVING SPACE(53). For those times when you do have formal meetings, you should have FORMAL SPACE(59).

Future rocket geeks.

58

Geek Space

. . . *in* LIVING SPACE(53) *we explained why banning the cubes in favor of more innovative solutions is a good idea, yet money and politics can prevent the best possible workspace from being created for the benefit of your team. Given the nature of many corporations today, autonomy in decision making is hard to come by. Often one must figure out how to make the best of a lousy situation.*

Even though you do not have the necessary political clout (or cash) to violate the ridiculous workspace doctrines handed down from some nameless vice president lurking somewhere in the corporate hierarchy, you still want to provide as stimulating an environment as possible given your resources.

Photograph by Diana Wright, © 2000. Used by permission.

Some developers hate cubes because they are isolating in nature, claustrophobic, and generally dehumanizing. There is even a service that will download the appropriate memorabilia for the person who will be sitting in the cube next. Some may like that of course, although we have never personally met anyone who does. It's a matter of one's personal taste, desire for solitude—even if it is a kind of pseudo-solitude—and enjoyment of sitting in one little spot throughout the day (see LIVING SPACE(53) and PRIVATE SPACE(56)). But what is the perfect geek-sized space? Is it possible to define a one-size-fits-all, or is that just demoting us all to living with the lowest common definition of the perfect cube? To paraphrase Albert Gore from his acceptance speech at the 2000 Democratic National Convention: "They're for the powerful and we're for the people!"

If all you have at your disposal are modular walls, identical chairs, and various sized desktops that hang off the walls, hand them over to your geeks. Don't bother hunting for a screwdriver; they already have plenty of those. As one well-known philosopher was wont to say, "Each according to his needs." Help your engineers meet their needs: For the social geeks who need a discussion and a little catch-up while they wait for their coffee to kick in, let them form a bullpen of cubes. We've seen foursomes, with short walls serving as the psychological demarcation between spaces. And then there are those who enjoy a duplex with one complementing the other, and there are always those who prefer darkness and solitude. They would lunge at the chance to outfit an old closet to their needs—hip-hop music, black light posters, and the comforting glow of an oversized monitor. It may not be possible to meet everyone's specific needs, but you are faced with more of an opportunity than a crisis: It's time for some collaboration, a *Geek Space Extravaganza*. Take it off-site for lunch or for an afternoon over beers. Maybe bring in a funky architect who can introduce new ideas about living and workspaces. Get a stack of books from the library that discuss building livable spaces. We think Christopher Alexander's *A Pattern Language* is a great place to start.

This is not a competitive affair, and authority is not doled out based on position or bulk of paycheck. Don't reserve the natural light for those who've put in 25 years, thereby creating an artificial pecking order. People have different needs, and if your old-timers haven't figured out how to manage their own exigencies by now, it sure isn't up to you to sort out their deeper problems. (In fact, it may be your old-timers who are really going to balk at this newest idea of yours. If they don't come, don't give them a voice in the ultimate decision.) Find out how much space you have to work with—lay out the dimensions on the white board; count up the number of walls, windows, and desktops available for your project; and let them work it out. If one developer wants a private cube, let her have it—she doesn't have to defend herself if that's what she wants. If they all want private cubes, let them have them (although, this should make you worry slightly about the level of risk this team can tolerate.) If they want to arrange their desks in one big circle that reminds you of your second-grade classroom, let them do it. If one malcontent wants four closed sides and a rope ladder to climb in every morning, fine.

This is not a dramatic interpretation of *Lord of the Flies,* and hopefully you won't allow it to play out in that manner.

If your team can't cooperatively determine how to live together, how will they ever cooperate when it comes to the designing and construction of complex software systems?

If your developers are immature whiners or carry a history of backstabbing and political maneuvering, you probably need to look at the ROTTEN FRUIT(46) before engaging in this exercise. It is also possible that your team will see this as an opportunity to exercise THE GAUNTLET(25) on some unsuspecting member of the team, but we say let it rip. The sooner your weak links are exposed, the better off everyone is.

Now it's time to build it. If you don't have a policy that mandates who snaps the modular furniture together, then each member of the team should oversee the construction of his or her new home. Otherwise, they should be present as the modular furniture experts do their thing. In fact, given the propensity toward clumsiness we've seen among some of our fellow developers, this might be preferable. The last thing you need is Human Resources asking you why your team's Worker's Compensation claims have soared. Each detail of the construction should be met with their satisfaction, and further decorative effects can be handled individually or with the cooperation of any cube-sharing parties.

Allow them to live with their new configuration for a while, and then revisit the situation in a few months to see how it's working. When it's time to raze it and start over, you'll know it. Who knows? Configurations could change as often as the demands of the next project. Of course, your technical support organization and facilities group will despise you for the wire and phones they have to move every time your team institutes a physical reorganization, but that's for you to sort out. Smaller negotiations might take place among individuals, and a wall might go up or down here or there, and that is totally acceptable. The fundamental point of this exercise is to allow your software developers to have some control over their everyday circumstances and to exercise their capabilities for cooperation with the team members upon whom they must rely and trust.

Therefore:
Give your software development team the opportunity to design and build workspaces that fit their varied needs, desires, and requirements. Allow them to cooperatively design the most innovative workspace they can conjure given the resources granted within the corporate confines.

GEEK SPACE(58) is closely related to UNIQUE PLACE(54). If you think we're making this up, we're not. One of the authors worked in knocked-off environments for years, living with scrounged furniture, partitions, walls, coffee machines, you name it. It was the best working environment he ever had.

An auditorium.

59

Formal Space

There is fortune in these simple halls,
Where commonest throngs assembled for Doges to proclaim.
Those crowns lie buried now beneath the walls,
While ancient spirit and living flesh of the Demos still remains,
As the constant blessing to the space contained.

Cardon Stimson

*. . . people gather to hear the news, to demonstrate solidarity, to air griev-
ances, or simply to be entertained.*

Formal presentations in which the entire organization is to be included are
sometimes necessary. A large comfortable space is difficult to maintain with
such infrequent utility, yet its existence serves an essential function.

*Photograph by Marion Post Wolcott, between 1935 and 1942; Library of Congress, Prints &
Photographs Division, FSA-OWI Collection [LC-USF33-030792-M5 DLC].*

Even with e-mail, the World Wide Web, and teleconferencing, every organization has the occasional need to present a program to a large number of people at the same time. Guest speakers may need such a space, or quarterly financial presentations may be given as a courtesy to employees. We know of one company whose employees have put on musical comedy productions about the company for the pleasure of all. A formal place that can act as a lecture forum, a playhouse, or a theater for interactive discourse is essential to any organization of more than a few dozen people.

Providing an auditorium or large formal space set aside for special use is often like having a dead zone. It is often well appointed, and there is some attempt to make it comfortable or possibly even beautiful, but nothing really happens there. It is often an ambiguous space that people would not naturally wander into for any normal activity. With some forethought into the cross-functional purposes of such a space, it is possible to provide for a formal setting that also becomes part of the everyday LIVING SPACE(53). One way to accommodate this is to provide for the space in a sunny place in the building that is surrounded by the GEEK SPACE(58) of your employees. The space, of course, will need to be flexible enough to allow a speaker to be comfortably viewed by a sizable crowd. It's not necessary to have permanent seating, as people can roll in their own chairs, or sit in chairs or in comfortable seats that are part of the overall LIVING SPACE(53) you have already established.

Therefore:
Provide a space that can be used as an auditorium within easy access of all office spaces. In should be able to hold at least an eighth to a quarter of the people in your organization at one time, but if it can hold all of them, make it convertible to other uses so that the space does not sit idle too much of the time. Equip this space with the various media devices that are required for presentations, question-and-answer sessions, and entertainment events.

One great barrista at a favorite hangout.

60

Fuel

. . . although some prefer their caffeine delivery systems to be something other than coffee, and a strange few avoid the substance altogether, the fact is that caffeine is easily the drug of choice for software developers. We just wonder: Have you had a really good cup of coffee from your company's cafeteria lately? Does that coffee machine with the little window of old beans dispense the black ambrosia you desire?[1]

Developers depend on coffee to fuel them in the morning, when they get the late-afternoon blahs, late in the night, and whenever they need a meaningful break to clear the pathways for new inspiration. In spite of this need, it is rare

---

1. If you're a tea drinker, or use soft drinks, or abstain from caffeine altogether, then read on just for amusement at the plight of the coffee-addicted. Also, if you work in Sweden, this probably won't apply either. The Swedes seem to really understand the need for *great* coffee in the workplace. Ah, Stockholm!

to get a really good cup of coffee from the local corporate dispensary even during the day. In the odd hours when developers need it most, there's nowhere to go.

"Coffee is recommended against the Contagion."—G. Harvey, Advice Against the Plague, *1665*

Could a good cup of coffee be called a *right* by the developer community? We think so, and not just because we are confirmed coffee addicts ourselves. It isn't just the drink. Although good coffee has powerful effects both physically and psychologically, we also enjoy the way it can punctuate the tedium and relieve the frustration that accompanies intense software development. It truly is a pause that refreshes, restores, and rejuvenates. Unless . . .

Unless it is the watery, bland dishwater that passes for coffee as it sits degrading in giant steel urns or boils slowly down to gelatinous muck in a drip pot over the hours of the day. If it is the sputum that dribbles out from a vending machine into a paper cup, heaven alone knows what *really* is in there, although the mummified carcass of a cockroach in the little display of "Real Coffee Beans" from which it was allegedly made should give you more than a clue. Add the simulated brewing sounds while waiting for the silt that gets churned out, and it turns what should be a pleasant break into just one more thing that has gone wrong. As you stand holding the abomination-filled paper cup, you consider that the best thing to do next is to begin a one-person assault on the entire industrialized world, starting with this machine. By the time you get back to your computer, your gut aches from the acid, and your mouth feels like it's been used to bathe the socks of the Russian army. The fact that you've been coding for 16 hours straight and skipped a couple of meals makes the moment a perfect substitute for hell.

Some companies have heeded this need and have added actual coffee bars to their facilities. This is great, and the ideal is a 24-hour on-premises coffeehouse complete with knowledgeable and skilled barrista. We do understand, however, that this is a little or a lot extreme, depending on your resources, size, and so on. But there are other ways.

Years ago, one of the authors worked in a facility like this (and aren't they *all?*), and he and his colleagues, coffee addicts all, decided to do something about it. One of them managed to procure a piston-driven espresso maker, its chrome and white enamel exterior gleaming like the best expectations of the dawning of the Machine

Age. Another brought in good beans and a grinder with which to get the perfect granularity through which to force steam and create delight. Each practiced with the machine until pulling a good espresso, or diluting it down to the perfect *Americano,* was as natural as setting a trap to find a memory leak. Several times a day, they would gather for a communal break and chat, each waiting on the others in a ceremony that achieved ritual status. If they were working late together, these meetings became even more valuable as they fueled themselves on overnighters and weekend marathons. Productivity noticeably increased, as did morale, and the smell of freshly pulled espresso filled the pathways like a siren song. Their manager, a soda drinker primarily, was puzzled but could see the benefits so he saw them through the crisis brought on by a misguided fire marshal who, upon inspection, couldn't figure out what the hell the thing was but was sure it was dangerous. The director of the facility thought the whole engineering coffee cult very weird until the engineers made him one of their concoctions, and he never visited the dreaded drip-maker again. The engineering team, Brothers and Sisters of the Bean, became the most respected group in the corporate software engineering organization. Coincidence? Perhaps. But if you were their manager, would you chance damage by putting them back on the bad stuff?

So we put to you the question: Are you doing anything to bring the coffee lovers the brew that they crave, that they need, that they deserve?

> Therefore:
> Whether by going all out and building a roaster right in your office, or by simply budgeting some petty cash for a consumer machine and the beans to supply it, provide the caffeine lovers on your staff with the real thing. They'll love you for it.

The use of this pattern is easily extended to the concept of nutrition via some delivery mechanism other than the vending machines so prevalent in the high-tech world. The key is to make sure that your developers know you respect their right to enjoy the experience of a decent cup of coffee and a fresh meal.

Care for a bite?

Letting time just flow. West Clear Creek, Arizona.

61

Vacation

. . . in the 52 weeks of each year, each contains 168 hours, at least 40 of which are spent working in software development and at least 20 more are devoted to getting ready for work and commuting to and from the workplace. Of the remaining hours, there are sleeping and eating, being with friends and family, and attending to life administration. Of course, nobody in this field works 40 hours, so the remaining waking hours devoted to life are even less. Home and regeneration time are fragmented and fit into whatever time is left over from work. True relaxation, rejuvenation, and inner renewal must come from vacations.

The typical allotment of vacation time in the United States of two or three weeks per year is both insulting and unhealthy.

Photograph by Don S. Olson, © 2000. All rights reserved.

Our European readers are most likely chuckling to themselves over this one. Five- or six-week leaves are the norm in Europe and are considered a fundamental entitlement to the worker. Think about it: Can you really take a meaningful vacation in two weeks, and if you do jam your entire vacation into two weeks to accommodate the school vacation schedule, is that really enough to renew a person or a family only once per year? Do you really believe that newer people in your company are in less need of the powers of rejuvenation than those who accrue time at a faster rate? Are they physically different? Mentally more resilient? Has it ever occurred to anyone in your "Human Resources" department that vacations are not some kind of benevolent gift but rather a health benefit, and they should not even be classified as a "benefit" but as a fundamental right of all workers?

Nope. Guess not. It's all about the bottom line, heads, necks, staffing profiles, yadda, yadda, yadda. Although your human resources department may not be tracking these numbers, there seems to be a trend toward earlier and earlier retirement for many people in technology. For others, cutting to part-time or freelance consulting is an attractive alternative to working 50 of 52 weeks every year. Attempts to give people a bit more time pop up here and there, but they are mostly pretty feeble attempts. Unpaid leaves of absence, buying additional vacation, or allowing a sabbatical of six weeks every seven years are offered, as if the company is doing the employee a huge favor by being so flexible. Again, let us reiterate—vacations are not a privilege, they are a right!!

When we were kids in school, there were Christmas vacations and spring break and summer vacations. In college, there were similar breaks that made possible the intense cramming sessions, the full load of classes, and the wild parties all through the nights. Then we went to our first job, and it slowly sank in that we had been had—but good. Two weeks' vacation, 9 or 10 holidays a year, and that's it. Get into harness, learn the lockstep, say goodbye to adventures and to learning new things outside of technology. You wanted to go dig for relics in Guatemala? Sorry. You thought about a trek along the spine of the Rocky Mountains living with only what you can carry and learning about what you carry inside you and what nature carries all around you? Too bad. You'd like to learn how your ancestors navigated from Iceland to Newfoundland in open boats by actually doing it as part of a crew on a replicated Viking longboat? Forget about it! Given your measly two weeks a year, you're going to spend at least half that just doing things that require a day or half-day here and there to take care of normal personal business. With that one remaining week, do you think you're going to really be able to disengage from work? Can you reconnect to the rest of life in a way that deepens you and your ability to bring value to your employer as a rested, focused individual? Screw that! You're part of the workforce now! You have no life.

Woodstock, Vermont, has nine ski tows and is generally very crowded with skiers on weekends.

Stingy vacations increase the rate of burnout and the resentment of those who give their all when they are on the job. Additionally, "busting back" people to the minimum vacation allotment every time they change jobs, or are "acquired," is no way to attract good people. In fact, those with the knowledge and skill to go out on their own often cite the parsimonious vacation policies of potential employers as why they prefer to work under their own auspices. Never, ever, have we heard of someone complaining of being too relaxed and focused on the job, the fault of which was having too much vacation. Certainly, there are those odd sorts who accumulate huge stores of vacation and take pride in never having a day off, or who have so totally succumbed to the idea of the primacy of the job that they fear being away more than one week, and pale even at that. These are victims of the current system (or themselves), not reasons to continue it.

Photograph by Marion Post Wolcott, 1939 or 1940; Library of Congress, Prints & Photographs Division, FSA-OWI Collection [LC-USF33-030787-M4 DLC].

Therefore:
Fight for, finagle, and through any means possible strive to change your company's policy on vacations. In the meantime, find a way to help your people get the time they need, despite your company's formal policy, through the liberal use of compensation time. Lobby your local and national representatives to pass legislation that mandates reasonable minimums that are based on age so that "busting back" is eliminated.

Don and Carol's List of Culturally Relevant or Iconic Artifacts

Total Commitment (2)

Dr. Strangelove: Or, How I Learned to Stop Worrying and Love the Bomb (film)—No one knows total commitment like General Jack D. Ripper. Okay, so it resulted in the "doomsday shroud" covering the earth and killing everything that didn't make it to a mineshaft.

The Magnificent Seven (film)—An American version of *The Seven Samurai* in which a commitment to principle over money and self-preservation makes a difference.

The Wild Bunch (film)—A total commitment by the director Sam Peckinpah and by the characters in the film. Despite their outlaw nature, they do the right thing. They all die in the end.

Leviathan (3)

Moby Dick, Herman Melville (book)—One of the authors' favorite books of all time, it contains observations about every human tendency and folly, and the endless permutations of man's relationship to the divine and eternal.

Drawing by Universalia Jane, © 2001. All rights reserved.

259

Howl, Allen Ginsberg (poem)—just because it swallows you whole, full of hidden illusion and allusion.

Leaves of Grass, Walt Whitman (book of poetry)—Life as Leviathan.

Drama (4)

The Heart Aroused: Poetry and the Preservation of the Soul in Corporate America, David Whyte (book)—Something beyond the money and the fame.

An Actor Prepares, Constantin Stanislavsky (book)—We're all actors on one level or another, so why not be as true as we can be?

Who's Afraid of Virginia Woolf with Elizabeth Taylor and Richard Burton (film)— Now this is drama of a sort you hope you do not find in the workplace.

Metaphor (5)

The Power of Myth, Joseph Campbell (books)—Campbell's books help connect us to the eternal themes of our humanity.

Switzerland (6)

Why Switzerland, Jonathon Steinberg (book)

Whole People (8)

To Kill a Mockingbird, Harper Lee (book)—Think of the whole person Boo Radley reveals himself to be.

Cultural Competence (9)

Read or watch a movie about someone who is not like you. The following two books are quite likely to be from a point of view very different from your own:

Black Elk Speaks, as told through John G. Neihardt

The Fire Next Time, James Baldwin

Blowhole (11)

The *I Ching* (book)—HOVER SHOES (10) for everyday living

Physics for Poets, Richard March (book)

Collected Poems, Langston Hughes (book)

Geek Channeling (12)

Read Shirley MacLaine's books, study Ramtha, and peruse a little Edgar Cayce to get some idea of channeling if you've never tried it. Hang out in Sedona, Arizona.

Exhibitionism (13)

Study the story of the American General George Patton who thoroughly understood exhibitionism. Or watch the *Godfather* series; dropping a severed horse head in an unsuspecting individual's bed is pretty dramatic and certainly makes a profound point.

Shameless Ignoramus (14)

The Good Soldier Schweik, Jaroslav Hasek (book, and also a great pub in Stockholm, Sweden)—Schweik is an artist of ignorance, and he survives World War I by appearing much dumber than he really is.

Colossus of Maroussi, Henry Miller (book)—Miller writes a travelogue and history of Greece while remaining wonderfully ignorant of it all.

Too Clever by Half (15)

A Shot in the Dark (film)—Stars Peter Sellers as Inspector Clouseau, the antigenius!

Houdini!!! The Career of Ehrich Weiss by Kenneth Silverman (book)

Forty Whacks (16)

The American television serial, *Leave It to Beaver*

Evita: The Real Life of Eva Peron, Nicholas Fraser and Marysa Navarro (book)

Hitler's Pope: The Secret History of Pius XII, John Cornwell (book)

Tribal Language (17)

The Autobiography of Red Cloud: War Leader of the Ogalalas, R. Eli Paul (book)

Online Jargon Dictionary: http://www.nightflight.com/foldoc/index.html

Social Jester (18)

Confessions of a Failed Southern Lady, Florence King (book)

Any Woody Allen comedy—Woody doing an imitation of Woody is irresistibly funny but gives him credibility when it counts.

Patch Adams (film)—a doctor in a red nose and big shoes demonstrates the power of laughter.

Direct Action (19)

Das Boot (film)—The captain of the U-boat is a compelling direct actor.

Deliver Us from Evil: An Interpretation of American Prohibition, Norman H. Clark (book)

People:

John Brown, American abolitionist

General Jack D. Ripper (from *Dr. Strangelove, or How I learned to Stop Worrying and Love the Bomb*)—Not a good example, exactly, but certainly a no-bull follow-through type person without regard for the consequences.

Martin Luther King, Junior

Leonard Peltier—A Native American activist who has served over a quarter century in prison for the murder of an FBI agent after a shoot-out on the Pine Ridge Indian Reservation in 1975. Many consider him innocent of the crime, including Amnesty International.

Oscar Schindler

And DIRECT ACTION(19) without a conscience:

Adolf Hitler

Augusto Pinochet, Chilean dictator

Charles Manson

. . . and one who failed to act directly in time—*Hamlet.*

Outcome Based (20)

Undaunted Courage, Stephen Ambrose (book)—Story of the Lewis and Clark Corps of Discovery at the beginning of the 1800s.

The Agony and the Ecstasy, Irving Stone (book)

Chariots of Fire (film)

Get a Guru (21)

Apollo 13, Jim Lovell and Jeffrey Kluger (book)

Einstein's Dreams, Alan P. Lightman (book)

Home Field Advantage (22)

Check out the Olympics the next time they're on the tube, and note how you feel when your country wins a gold. Watch the athletes' faces; listen to your national anthem. You might get teary-eyed, even if you're a major anarchist.

Or, turn on your local sports coverage.

Overtime Detox (23)

Nudist on the Late Shift, Po Bronson (book)—Tales from the tech boom of the 1990s.

Defense De Pisser (24)

Smoke and Mirrors: The War on Drugs and the Politics of Failure, Dan Baum (book)

Drug War Politics: The Price of Denial, Eva Bertram with Kenneth Sharpe and Peter Andreas (book)

The Gauntlet (25)

Stalag 17 (film)—A film by Billy Wilder. In the end, a traitor exposed through a gauntlet of sorts.

Push the Customer (26)

The Myth of Sisyphus, Albert Camus (book)

Finish Line (27)

Any book on racing technique.

The story of Moses leading the Israelites—40 years in the desert and no finish line?

History of the World, Part 1 (film)—A film by Mel Brooks with an alternative view.

Inoculation (28)

An Inquiry into the Causes and Effects of the Variolae Vaccinae, a Disease Discovered in Some of the Western Counties of England, Particularly Gloucestershire, and Known by the Name of Cow Pox, Edward Jenner.

One by One (31)

It Takes a Village, Hillary Clinton (book)

The motto of the United States of America: *E Pluribus Unum* ("From many, one")

Train Hard, Fight Easy (32)

Observe any sporting team at practice. Similarly, military training operations and even civilian flight training will display a similar philosophy.

Trial Project (33)

Attend an exhibition game for your favorite sport, take flying lessons, or learn to spar.

Defeat (35)

Study the lives of Nelson Mandela and Winston Churchill.

Recall the 1955 Brooklyn Dodgers.

Recall learning to ride a bicycle.

Spanish Ounce of Gold (37)

Moby Dick, Herman Melville (book)

The Holy Grail, Norma Lorre Goodrich (book)

The Wealth of Nations, Adam Smith (book)

Significant Events (38)

The People's History of the United States, Howard Zinn (book)

Herding Cats (39)

Eyes on the Prize, the American Public Broadcasting System television series about the Civil Rights movement in the United States.

Divide and Conquer (40)

Soldier of Fortune (magazine)—A publication of real and aspiring mercenaries.

Passengers Push (42)

Check out Extreme Programming on the web at the following addresses:

- ◆ http://www.extremeprogramming.org
- ◆ http://c2.com/cgi/wiki?ExtremeProgrammingRoadmap

Decipher Discontent (43)

Mutiny on the Bounty (film)—The one with Charles Laughton and Clark Gable is preferable, followed by the version with Marlon Brando. If the other two are checked out, wait for their return rather than settle for Mel Gibson.

Backfires (44)

Investigate the similarities and differences between the Los Alamos fire in New Mexico and the Pumpkin fire in Arizona's Kendrick Peak Wilderness in the summer of 2000. See:

- http://www.fs.fed.us/r3/coconino/fire_pumpkin.shtml
- http://www.hcn.org/2000/jul03/dir/Essay__Los_Alamos.html

Rotten Fruit (46)

DDT, the now generally outlawed, but highly effective, pesticide.

Featurectomy (47)

http://my.webmd.com/content/asset/adam_disease_appendicitis

Cargo Cult (49)

Cargo Cults: Strange Stories of Desire from Melanesia and Beyond, Lamont Lindstrom (book)

This is Spinal Tap (film)—Just wait for the scene about their amplifier—it goes to 11!

Cop a Plea (50)

A Tale of Two Cities, Charles Dickens (book)

All the President's Men, Robert Woodward and Carl Bernstein (book)

Abandon Ship (52)

The Perfect Storm: A True Story of Men Against the Sea, Sebastian Junger (book)

Any of the thousands of books about the *Titanic* disaster

Living Space (53)

A Pattern Language, Christopher Alexander (book)

Unique Place (54)

How Buildings Learn: What Happens After They're Built, Stewart Brand (book)

The Timeless Way of Building, Christopher Alexander (book)

Ball Court (55)

Indians of the American Southwest, Steven L. Walker (book)

Private Space (56)

The Electronic Frontier Foundation: http://www.eff.org

American Civil Liberties Union: http://www.aclu.org/

1984, George Orwell (book)—A world in which privacy is a crime.

Fuel (60)

Zagats guide to dining

Go to a fine dining establishment, and have a fabulous meal with fine wine and a café crème to follow. It's on us. Yeah, right.

Vacation (61)

Take a vacation, and while on it rent any Elvis movie where he goes to the beach, or rent *Mr. Hobbes Takes a Vacation* with Jimmy Stewart. Also, read:

The Overworked American: The Unexpected Decline of Leisure, Juliet B. Schor (book)

Bibliography

Books and Periodicals

Alexander, Christopher (1979). *The Timeless Way of Building*. New York: Oxford University Press (ISBN: 0195024028).

Alexander, Christopher (1975). *A Pattern Language*. New York: Oxford University Press (ISBN: 0195019199).

Ambrose, Stephen (1996). *Undaunted Courage: Meriwether Lewis, Thomas Jefferson, and the Opening of the American West*. New York: Simon & Schuster (ISBN: 0684811073).

Anonymous (1995, Feb. 1). *Three Mile Island,* Earth Explorer.

Baldwin, James (1995). *The Fire Next Time*. New York: Modern Library (ISBN: 0679601511).

Baum, Dan (1997). *Smoke and Mirrors: The War on Drugs and the Politics of Failure*. Boston: Little, Brown and Company (ISBN: 0316084468).

Baynes, C.F. (1967). *The I Ching or Book of Changes*. (R. Wilhelm and Vary F. Baynes, Trans.). Princeton, NJ: Princeton University Press (ISBN: 069109750X).

Beck, Kent (2000). *eXtreme Programming Explained*. Reading, MA: Addison-Wesley (ISBN: 0201616416).

Bernstein, Carl, and Woodward, Robert (1994). *All the President's Men.* Carmichael, CA: Touchstone Books (ISBN: 0671894412).

Bertram Eva, Sharpe, Kenneth, and Andreas, Peter (1996). *Drug War Politics: The Price of Denial.* Berkeley: University of California Press (ISBN: 0520205987).

Black Elk and Neihardt, John G. (2000). *Black Elk Speaks.* Lincoln: University of Nebraska Press (ISBN: 0803213093).

Blanton, Brad (1996). *Radical Honesty: How to Transform Your Life by Telling the Truth.* New York: Dell Trade Paperback (ISBN: 0440507545).

Brand, Stewart (1995). *How Buildings Learn: What Happens After They're Built.* New York: Penguin USA (ISBN: 0140139966).

Bronson, Po (1999). *Nudist on the Late Shift.* New York: Random House (ISBN: 0375502777).

Brown, William J., Malveau, Raphael C., Brown, William H., McCormick, Hays W. III, and Mowbray, Thomas J. (1998). *AntiPatterns.* New York: John Wiley & Sons (ISBN: 0471197130).

Campbell, Joseph (1988). *The Power of Myth.* New York: Doubleday (0385247745).

Camus, Albert (1991). *The Myth of Sisyphus.* New York: Vintage Books (ISBN: 0679733736).

Chopra, Deepak (1994). *The Seven Spiritual Laws of Success.* San Rafael, CA: Amber-Allen Publishing and New World Library (ISBN: 1878424114).

Clark, Norman H. (1985). *Deliver Us from Evil: An Interpretation of American Prohibition.* New York: W.W. Norton & Company (ISBN: 0393091708).

Cleary, Thomas (2001). *Classics of Strategy and Counsel: The Art of Wealth, Living a Good Life, the Human Element, Back to Beginnings.* Boston, MA: Shambhala Publications (ISBN: 1570627290).

Clinton, Hillary (1996). *It Takes a Village.* New York: Simon & Schuster (ISBN: 0684818434).

Constantine, Larry (1995). *Constantine on Peopleware.* Englewood Cliffs, NJ: Prentice Hall/Yourdon Press (ASIN: 0133319768).

Cooper, Alan (1999). *The Inmates are Running the Asylum: Why High Tech Products Drive Us Crazy and How to Restore the Sanity.* Indianapolis, IN: Sams (ISBN: 0672316498).

Coplien, James O. (1996). *Software Patterns.* Cambridge, MA: SIGS Books and Multimedia, AT&T, 1996 (ISBN: 188484250X)

Cornwell, John (2000). *Hitler's Pope: The Secret History of Pius XII.* New York: Penguin USA (ISBN: 0140296271).

DeSalvo, Tina (1999, June 1). Unleash the creativity in your organization. *HR Magazine.*

Dickens, Charles (1997). *A Tale of Two Cities.* New York, New American Library (ISBN: 0451526562).

Easton, Mark (1991, Jan. 1). *Papua New Guinea: Chapter 3. Postindependence.* Countries of the World.

Fraser, Nicholas, and Navarro, Marysa (1996). *Evita: The Real Life of Eva Peron.* New York: W.W. Norton & Company (ISBN: 0393315754).

Gamma, Erich, Helm, Richard, Johnson, Ralph, and Vlissides, John (1995). *Design Patterns: Elements of Reusable Object-Oriented Software.* Reading, MA: Addison-Wesley (ISBN: 0201633612).

Ginsberg, Allen (1991). *Howl and Other Poems.* San Francisco: City Lights Books (ISBN: 0872860175).

Goodrich, Norma Lorre (1993). *The Holy Grail.* New York: Harper Perennial Library (ISBN: 0060922044).

Gordon, Thomas (1977). *Leader Effectiveness Training.* New York: G. P. Putnam's Sons (ISBN: 0399128883).

Graham, John. *Drug Abuse Prevention: Beyond "Just Say No."* From Health and Human Development on-line magazine (www.hhdev.psu.edu/research/rsrch.htm).

Harvey, G. (1665). *Advice Against the Plague.*

Hasek, Jaroslav (1985). *The Good Soldier Schweik.* New York: Viking Press (ISBN: 0140182748).

Jenner, Edward (1798). *An Inquiry into the Causes and Effects of the Variolae Vaccinae, a Disease Discovered in Some of the Western Counties of England, Particularly Gloucestershire, and Known by the Name of Cow Pox.* Self-published at http://www.jennermuseum.com.

Junger, Sebastian (1997). *The Perfect Storm: A True Story of Men Against the Sea,* New York: W.W. Norton & Company (ISBN: 0393050327).

King, Florence (1990). *Confessions of a Failed Southern Lady.* New York: St. Martin's Press (ISBN: 0312050631).

Lee, Harper (1960). *To Kill A Mockingbird.* New York: HarperCollins (ISBN: 0060194995).

Leifer, Eric M. (1995, Sept. 1). Perverse effects of social support: Publics and performance in major league sports. *Social Forces.*

Levine, Rick, Locke, Christopher, Searls, Doc, and Weinberger, David (2000). *The Cluetrain Manifesto.* Cambridge, MA: Perseus Books (ISBN: 0738202444).

Lightman, Alan P. (1993). *Einstein's Dreams.* New York: Pantheon Books (ISBN: 0679416463).

Lindstrom, Lamont (1993). *Cargo Cults: Strange Stories of Desire from Melanesia and Beyond.* Honolulu: University of Hawaii Press (ISBN: 0824815262).

Lovell Jim, and Kluger, Jeffrey (1996). *Apollo 13.* New York: Pocket Books (ISBN: 0671534645).

March, Richard (1995). *Physics for Poets.* New York: McGraw-Hill (ISBN: 0070402485).

MacLaine, Shirley (1984). *Out on a Limb.* New York: Bantam (out of print) (ISBN: 0553273701)

McConnell, Steve (1996). *Rapid Development.* Redmond, WA: Microsoft Press (ISBN: 1556159005).

Melville, Herman (1992). *Moby Dick.* New York: Modern Library (ISBN: 0679600108).

Miller, Henry (1988). *The Colossus of Maroussi.* New York: W.W. Norton & Company (ISBN: 0811201090).

Miller, Henry (1961). *Tropic of Cancer.* New York: Grove Press (ISBN: 0802131786).

Nelson, Walter Henry (1969). *The Berliners.* New York: David McKay Company (ASIN: 0582127807).

Olson, Dave (1993). *Exploiting Chaos.* New York: Van Nostrand Reinhold (ASIN: 0442011121).

Orwell, George (1990). *1984.* New York: New American Library Classics (ISBN: 0451524934).

Paul, R. Eli (Ed.), Red Cloud, Deon, Sam, and Allen, Charles Wesley (1997). *The Autobiography of Red Cloud: War Leader of the Oglalas.* Helena: Montana Historical Society (ISBN: 0917298500).

Ramtha (1986). *I Am Ramtha.* Hillsboro, OR: Beyond Words Publishing Company (ISBN: 0896100049).

Schor, Juliet B. (1993). *The Overworked American: The Unexpected Decline of Leisure.* New York: Basic Books (ISBN: 046505434X).

Shakespeare, William (1980). *Hamlet* from *The Complete Works of William Shakespeare,* third edition, David Bevington, editor. Glenview, IL: Scott, Foresman, and Company (ISBN: 067315193X).

Silverman, Kenneth (1997). *Houdini!!! The Career of Ehrich Weiss.* New York: Harper Perennial Library (ISBN: 006092862X).

Smith, Adam (2000). *The Wealth of Nations.* New York: Modern Library (ISBN: 0679783369).

Soldier of Fortune (magazine).

Stanislavsky, Constantin (1948). *An Actor Prepares.* New York: Theatre Arts (ISBN: 0878309837).

Stearn, Jess (1990). *Edgar Cayce—The Sleeping Prophet.* New York: Bantam Books (ISBN: 0553260855).

Steinberg, Jonathan (1996). *Why Switzerland.* Cambridge, UK: Cambridge University Press (ISBN: 0521484537).

Stewart, Thomas A. (1997). *Intellectual Capital.* New York: Doubleday (ISBN: 0385482280).

Stone, Irving (1996). *The Agony and the Ecstasy.* New York: New American Library (ISBN: 0451171357).

Sun Tzu (1963). *The Art of War.* Oxford, UK: Oxford University Press (ISBN: 0195014766).

United States Nuclear Regulatory Commission, *A Short History of Nuclear Regulation, 1946–1999.* http://www.nrc.gov/SECY/smj/shorthis.htm.

Walker, Steven L. (1994). *Indians of the American Southwest.* Scottsdale, AZ: Camelback Design Group (ISBN: 1879924099).

Whitman, Walt (1993). *Leaves of Grass.* New York: Modern Library (ISBN: 0679600760).

Whyte, David (1994). *The Heart Aroused: Poetry and the Preservation of the Soul in Corporate America.* New York: Currency-Doubleday (ISBN: 0385484186).

Zinn, Howard (1999). *The People's History of the United States.* New York: HarperCollins (ISBN: 0060194480).

Films

A Shot in the Dark. Directed and written by Blake Edwards, 1964, color, 101 mins.

Chariots of Fire. Directed by Hugh Hudson, written by Colin Welland, 1981, color, 123 mins.

Das Boot. Directed and written by Wolfgang Petersen, based on the novel by Lothar-Gunther Buchheim, 1982, color, 150 mins.

Dr. Strangelove: Or, *How I Learned to Stop Worrying and Love the Bomb.* Directed/cowritten by Stanley Kubrick, 1964, black and white, 93 mins.

The Godfather. Directed by Francis Ford Coppola. Screenplay by Francis Ford Coppola and Mario Puzo from Puzo's novel, 1972, color, 175 mins.

History of the World, Part I. Directed and written by Mel Brooks, 1981, color, 92 mins.

The Magnificent Seven. Directed by John Sturges, written by William Roberts, Walter Bernstein, and Walter Newman, based on *The Seven Samurai,* 1960, color, 126 mins.

Mr. Hobbs Takes a Vacation. Directed by Henry Koster, written by Nunnally Johnson, based on the book *Hobbs' Vacation* by Edward Streeter, 1962, color, 115 mins.

Mutiny on the Bounty. Directed by Lewis Milestone, written by Charles Lederer, 1962, color, 179 mins.

Mutiny on the Bounty. Directed by Frank Lloyd, written by Charles Nordhoff and James Norman Hall, 1935, black and white, 132 mins.

Patch Adams. Directed by Tom Shadyac, written by Steve Oedekerk, based on the book *Gesundheit, Good Health Is a Laughing Matter* by Hunter Doherty Adams and Maureen Mylander, 1998, color, 115 mins.

Stalag 17. Directed and written by Billy Wilder, 1953, black and white, 120 mins.

This Is Spinal Tap. Directed by Rob Reiner, written by Christopher Guest, Rob Reiner, Michael McKean, and Harry Shearer, 1984, color, 82 mins.

Who's Afraid of Virginia Woolf? Directed by Mike Nichols, written by Ernest Lehman, based on the play by Edward Albee, 1966, black and white, 131 mins.

The Wild Bunch. Directed by Sam Peckinpah, written by Walon Green and Sam Peckinpah, based on a story by Walon Green and Roy N. Sickner, 1969, color, 145 mins.

Index

Also Available from Addison-Wesley

Design Patterns
Elements of Reusable Object-Oriented Software
By Erich Gamma, Richard Helm, Ralph Johnson,
and John Vlissides
Addison-Wesley Professional Computing Series

Capturing a wealth of experience about the design of object-oriented software, four top-notch designers present a catalog of simple and succinct solutions to commonly occurring design problems. Previously undocumented, these twenty-three patterns allow designers to create more flexible, elegant, and ultimately reusable designs without having to rediscover the design solutions themselves.

0-201-63361-2 • Hardcover • 416 pages • ©1995

Pattern Hatching
By John Vlissides
Software Patterns Series

This succinct, example-driven book empowers software developers who are using design patterns—arguably today's most popular object-oriented programming concept. *Design Patterns* coauthor John Vlissides blends his intimate knowledge of the pattern development process with practical techniques for better pattern application. The result is a thought-provoking guide that will help you improve your next software design by putting patterns to work successfully.

0-201-43293-5 • Paperback • 192 pages • ©1998

Pattern Languages of Program Design 4
By Neil Harrison, Brian Foote, and Hans Rohnert
Software Patterns Series

The fourth volume in a series of books documenting patterns for professional software developers, *Pattern Languages of Program Design 4* represents the current and state-of-the-art practices in the patterns community. The twenty-nine chapters of this book were each presented at recent PLoP conferences and have been explored and enhanced by leading experts in attendance. Representing the best of the conferences, these patterns provide effective, tested, and versatile software design solutions for solving real-world problems in a variety of domains.

0-201-43304-4 • Paperback • 784 pages • ©2000

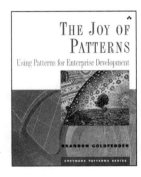

The Joy of Patterns
Using Patterns for Enterprise Development
By Brandon Goldfedder
Software Patterns Series

Take the struggle out of learning about design patterns! Through example-based teaching, *The Joy of Patterns* reveals the essence of design patterns as a higher-level language for describing system design. This book illustrates how to build more efficient, robust, and reusable designs with this powerful programming paradigm. Design patterns have been used as an integral technique for creating better software, and getting started with design patterns has never been easier!

0-201-65759-7 • Paperback • 208 pages • ©2002